healing
ancestral
family
patterns

healing ancestral family patterns

A Practical Guide to Ending the Cycle of Intergenerational Trauma

Dr. Steven Farmer

Hierophantpublishing

Cover design by Adrian Morgan
Cover art by Shutterstock
Print book interior design by Frame25 Productions

Hierophant Publishing
San Antonio, TX
www.hierophantpublishing.com

If you are unable to order this book from your local bookseller, you may order directly from the publisher.

Library of Congress Control Number: 2025932218
ISBN: 978-1-950253-63-0

10 9 8 7 6 5 4 3 2 1

If you look deeply into the palm of your hand, you will see your parents and all generations of your ancestors. All of them are alive in this moment. Each is present in your body. You are the continuation of each of these people.

—Thich Nhat Hanh, *Present Moment Wonderful Moment*

Contents

Introduction   1

Part I: Understanding Ancestral Family Patterns

Chapter 1: Exploring Your Ancestry   23

Chapter 2: Family Secrets   35

Chapter 3: The Dark Law   43

Chapter 4: Rewriting Ancestral Stories   53

Chapter 5: Messages from Your Ancestors   63

Part II: Healing Ancestral Family Patterns

Chapter 6: Channeling Forgiveness   79

Chapter 7: Healing Wounds and Trauma   87

Chapter 8: Shamanic Journeying   103

Chapter 9: Stepping Back   117

Chapter 10: Connecting with Ancestral Spirits   127

Chapter 11: Crossing Over   145

Chapter 12: Ancestral Messengers   161

Chapter 13: The Four Gifts   171

Chapter 14: Paying It Forward   181

Chapter 15: Spiritual and Territorial Ancestors   187

Conclusion   193

Acknowledgments   197

Appendix A: Therapeutic Modalities That Support
Ancestral Work   199

Appendix B: Addiction and 12-Step Programs   207

Appendix C: Index of Exercises   211

Resources   215

Introduction

I spent my early childhood in Iowa, but when I was twelve, my family moved to California. I didn't have any strong religious indoctrination, although we did go to church on occasion. Like many people raised in the United States, I didn't even think about my ancestors for much of my childhood. Even after my grandparents and parents died, I didn't think of them as "ancestors," nor did I think that way about any of my great-grandparents or even more distant relatives to whom I was biologically and spiritually connected. They were just dead relatives, plain and simple. Gone. No longer relevant to my life.

After completing degrees in psychology and psychotherapy, I eventually became licensed as a marriage and family therapist. Early on in my practice, I was struck by the fact that many of my clients' problems were in part the result of family dynamics, although at first I didn't look much beyond their immediate families. Over time, it became increasingly apparent to me that their early formative years and the nature of the families in which they grew up needed to be reckoned with in order for emotional and psychic healing to progress. But I still didn't consider the ways in which their extended family trees and the patterns they contained were influencing their lives.

I continued my professional training in family systems, hypnotherapy, gestalt therapy, and a variety of other modalities. In addition, I did my own inner work, exploring many avenues for behavioral, emotional, and psychic healing. Then in 1990, I began to study shamanism with teachers from a wide range of traditions, from Tibetan to Celtic and everything in between. All of my shamanic teachers emphasized the idea that our ancestors are an active presence in our lives. That was when everything clicked for me. I began to incorporate ancestral healing into my daily spiritual practice and to teach it to my clients—with extraordinary results.

Ancestral Family Patterns

Ancestral family patterns are those physical, emotional, behavioral, and mental traits—both positive and negative—that you have inherited from your forebears and that you carry in your DNA and in your soul. Let's look at each of these categories in more detail.

Physical Traits

The physical traits you inherit from your ancestors include obvious characteristics like height, build, and eye color, but also predispositions to physical illnesses and injuries, and attitudes and habits pertaining to physical health. These physical family traits may manifest as:

- Refusing to get appropriate medical care when needed

- Hypochondria or malingering in illness as a way of avoiding the demands of life

- Taking unnecessary risks that result in frequent injuries

- Overeating as a bulwark against potential future hunger

- "Eating like a bird" or having little interest in food

- A tendency to suffer from headaches, colds, heart disease, or other specific illnesses

- Being prone to preventable illnesses due to lack of exercise or self-care

- Injuries that result from overwork, taking on too much, or trying to do it all yourself

- Dying young or living to old age

- Feeling grounded in your body or living in your head

- Seeing yourself as physically fragile or sturdy

Emotional Traits

Emotional traits are related to temperament. Did you inherit your grandmother's melancholy? Your father's quick temper? Did your whole clan love to tell jokes and stories? Common emotional family traits include:

- A tendency toward melancholy or depression

- Being socially withdrawn or gregarious

- Being hotheaded and quick to anger

- Punishing others by withdrawing emotionally

- Overwhelming others with outsized displays of emotion

- Repressing your emotions to keep the peace

- "Letting it all hang out" and speaking with no filter regardless of the consequences

- Experiencing intense jealousy, outrage, or contempt

- Being unable to feel or identify your emotions

Behavioral Traits

Behavioral traits govern the actions you take or refrain from taking. Are you a risk-taker, or do you play it safe? Do you find it easy to commit to relationships, or do you bounce from partner to partner? Behavioral traits may include:

- Workaholism, alcoholism, compulsive shopping, or other addictions

- A strong pull toward a certain career path or vocation

- A recurring pull toward the same game, sport, or hobby

- A tendency to save money and be frugal

- A pattern of spending money as soon as you have it

- Enduring marriages, divorces, abusive relationships, or unwanted pregnancies

- Strictness or leniency in child-rearing

- Abandonment, neglect, or abuse

- Tight-knit family relationships, or generations of sibling rivalries, rifts, and family feuds

- Banishment or exile

- Rootedness or frequent moves

Mental Traits

Mental traits influence the way you think and process information, as well as your specific beliefs and leanings. These may show up in your family tree as:

- Shared political, religious, or spiritual views

- Shared beliefs about gender roles and gender identity, or about sexuality and its expression

- A tendency toward anxiety

- Overconfidence or arrogance

- Self-doubt and self-sabotage

- A "mind like a steel trap" or a "memory like a sieve"

- Forgetfulness, fogginess

- Being a quick thinker or a dreamer with your head in the clouds

When taken together, these four categories of traits begin to describe recognizable patterns. Do members of your family have a habit of amassing great fortunes, only to squander them? Are they emotionally distant with their own children, but warm and affectionate with the children of others? Do they tend to steel themselves constantly against disasters that never come? Do they neglect their health until it's too late? Do they fail to control their anger? Do they refuse to apologize, even though it may cost them dear friendships and relationships?

Despite what these questions may imply, it is important to note that not all ancestral patterns are bad. As you contemplate your own ancestry, you will discover that many of the family traits you find there are worthy of being cherished and celebrated, and you will have opportunities to do so as you work through this book. My primary goal here is to help you heal patterns that are causing you undue distress or holding you back from optimum health, happiness, and connection. As you will soon see, when you do this healing work, the benefits flow backward and forward along your family tree, touching *everyone* in your family line—past, present, and future.

Ancestral Connections

Although there are different views on what an ancestor or an ancestral spirit is, everyone seems to agree that the term refers to a deceased person who dwells on "the other side"—just across the veil. Most people think of ancestors as those to whom they are biologically related, and that is completely valid. But in some cases, we may have connections with ancestors that go beyond our direct lineages: for example, in the case of adoption, or simply because we feel a strong resonance on a spiritual level.

Take a close look at the features of your face and compare them with those of your parents and, if possible, your grandparents. You may notice features or even physical maladies that echo the faces of these relatives.

And there is abundant evidence that our families live within us—both in our DNA and in our souls.

In her book *My Stroke of Insight,* neuroanatomist Jill Bolte Taylor claims that, in fact, 99.99 percent of human genetic sequencing is exactly the same. That means that only 0.01 percent of our DNA is responsible for making us the unique individuals we are! So truly, no matter what ethnic and cultural elaborations have formed us, we are all much more alike than we are different. Our body structures, our facial features, our skin color—the confluence of these and so many other factors came together miraculously to make us who we are. No one human being is like any other on this planet. Yet paradoxically, because of our DNA, we are all connected to every other human being.

To identify the characteristics of that 0.01 percent, we need only look to our most immediate genetically related ancestors—mother, father, grandmother, grandfather, etc. Genetically and spiritually, we're most strongly connected to relatives of the previous three generations, some of whom we probably knew while they were still living. We may not have known others, like our great-great-grandparents, but we may have heard stories about them.

When a baby is born, people often make comments like: "Oh, she looks like her father/mother/sister/brother." These family resemblances typically become more evident as the child matures. Moreover, that child retains within their genetic makeup not only the physical characteristics of these ancestors, but also their psychological and emotional predilections. In other words, our most immediate ancestors pass along more than just physical similarities; they also pass along their positive character traits, as well as their unhealthy and dysfunctional behaviors and patterns.

As we go back several generations, these connections may become less obvious as the gene pool becomes increasingly diffuse. The number of ancestors doubles every generation, starting with our parents. Ten generations back, the number of directly related ancestors rises to 1,024. Twenty generations back, it grows to 1,048,576! In fact, if we go back far enough, we find that we all share a common lineage. After all, we all started from the same gene pool. And although we are composed of genetic material most similar to those in our more immediate family line, other factors can influence our character and our personality as well. These are the patterns we will explore in this book.

These ancestral connections are an indelible part of our heritage. But the patterns that reside deep within them are not permanently ingrained. With conscientious effort, they can be modified and healed. This only requires that we be proactive and intentional in our efforts. Moreover, as Helen Schucman's *A Course in Miracles* tells us: "When I am healed, I am not healed alone" (Lesson 137). As you'll see, when you heal ancestral patterns through the methods described in this book, this healing goes backward to your ancestors—*and* forward to your descendants.

Words of Caution

In the following pages, I give you all the tools you need to heal the wounds of your ancestry, while tapping into its unique strengths. No matter how strong and intransigent your ancestral patterns may appear, rest assured that you can be the one to transform them, both for yourself and for the benefit of future generations.

Nonetheless, there are times when you should seek professional help before attempting an ancestral healing. While the aim of the practices in this book is to address any potential underlying causes related to a family pattern, some conditions may require an initial intervention from a qualified professional. These conditions include:

- Severe emotional upsets

- Life-threatening illnesses

- Grief from loss

- Frequent panic episodes

- Debilitating addictions

- Muscular tension from excessive stress

- Spiritual emergencies

If you are experiencing any of these conditions, please seek support and refer to the resources in the appendices at the back of this book for further suggestions.

Another caution I share concerns post-traumatic stress disorder, or PTSD, a condition characterized by nightmares, flashbacks, and chronic overactivation of the fight-or-flight response. Many people only become curious about this ancestral pattern after sharing the trauma of a family member or ancestor. A participant at one of my ancestral healing workshops endured incredible hardships as a toddler in a Nazi labor camp. One horrifying experience involved her grandmother having to sacrifice a child born in the camp in order to save other family members.

Many years later, this woman became pregnant with a child who was diagnosed with a condition that results in severe physical and mental disabilities. Faced with the heartbreaking choice of carrying the child to term or having a late-term abortion, she and her husband chose to "save the lives" of their two healthy daughters rather than allow their physical and emotional resources to be consumed with caring for a disabled child. It wasn't until she attended my workshop that this woman connected the dots between her grandmother's experience during the Holocaust and her own situation. When she realized that the trauma of losing a baby had repeated itself across generations, she understood that she was deeply connected to her grandmother's pain.

Many of us baby boomers have parents whose lives were irrevocably altered by World War II, whether they were soldiers, prisoners, orphans, or widows. Even if we were born *after* the war, the effects of this traumatic time may have lingered on in the form of a father's frightening outbursts, a mother's grief, or a grandfather's lifelong distrust of people from "the other side."

If your ancestors suffered through a war, a natural disaster, or some other highly stressful experience, they may have suffered from PTSD. In turn, you and your siblings may carry this pain as a result of having parents who lash out, shut down, abuse drugs and alcohol, or act in frightening or unpredictable ways.

Everyone responds differently to these situations, so the intensity of reactions can vary across individuals and also across a single lifetime, depending on other stressors or protective factors that may be present. There are four specific signs to look for to determine if your ancestral patterns include a history of PTSD—whether as a result of abuse, or war, or other violence. These are intrusive memories, avoidance, cynicism, and constant vigilance. Let's look briefly at each one so you can learn to recognize them in your own life.

Intrusive memories: When images and feelings from a traumatizing experience are retained in your mental, emotional, or physical memory, events or actions that resemble that trauma can trigger hallucinations, nightmares, and severe emotional distress. For example, if you grew up with an abusive parent, you may feel triggered by the sound of a slamming door or the scent of a certain cologne or hair product.

Avoidance: If you were abused or experienced other forms of extreme stress, you may consciously or unconsciously avoid places, people, and situations that remind you of the events and go to great lengths to stay "safe," even when this prevents you from taking part in everyday activities. Or you may deny the problem and try not to think or talk about it.

Cynicism: Traumatic experiences, especially those involving relatives or family members, can lead you to have a cynical view of the world and others. For example, if you watched your dad beat your mom, you may conclude that all men are violent and controlling, and avoid close relationships with them. You may even avoid all intimate relationships to protect yourself from being hurt.

Constant vigilance: This can manifest as difficulty sleeping or being easily startled. You may feel as if your nerves are on edge much of the time, or find yourself scanning the world for any signs of possible danger—even in situations that are quite safe. This can make it hard for you to focus at school or at work, and drain your mental and physical resources away from the ordinary tasks of life.

Although resources for managing PTSD used to be scarce, there are now many treatment modalities available to those who suffer from it. Before proceeding with the ancestral healing practices in this book, some of which can be quite intense, evaluate your own level of traumatization. If you are triggered in any of the ways described above, or if you suffer from frequent nightmares or flashbacks concerning family members, I suggest that you seek the guidance and support of a licensed counselor. You can always return to your healing path once your trauma symptoms are under control.

How to Use This Book

This book is organized into two parts. Part I explores the process of analyzing your family tree—taking stock of ancestral patterns, uncovering family secrets, discovering what I call your "dark law," examining the stories you tell about yourself and your ancestors, and receiving and interpreting the messages sent to you by your ancestors. I recommend that you read part I in its entirety before moving on to part II, which you can read in any order you like, turning to individual chapters as they call to you.

Part II introduces a wide range of practices for healing ancestral patterns. These are drawn from many different spiritual and therapeutic traditions, from shamanism to modern talk therapy. Although you may be familiar with some of these, don't be afraid to experiment with practices that fall outside your comfort zone. You may be surprised at how effective they are. Remember, the task of healing ancestral patterns isn't limited to one culture or tradition. All humans around the world are faced with this important work.

I strongly recommend that, before you begin this work, you commit to keeping a journal in which you write down your experiences and what you learn from the exercises that follow. Any type of notebook will do, as long as it is dedicated to your healing process. In it, record your dreams, your impressions, your communications with ancestors, and your healing experiences so that you can return to them and reflect on them later. This can be an invaluable tool as you journey down the path of ancestral healing.

Many of the exercises in this book are inspired by shamanism. When I use this word here, I am referring to more than just the Siberian tradition from which the word originated. Rather, I use it to describe the spiritual practices of Native peoples around the world that were common before the rise of modern religion. As you will see, these ancient healing practices have much to teach us about ancestral work, although they have been largely ignored by Western science.

That being said, it isn't necessary to pursue a shamanic path to enjoy the wealth of benefits you, your family, and your descendants can reap from an active and conscious relationship with your ancestors. Whether you're an atheist or a mystic, working with your ancestors can be an effective way to achieve healing and personal growth. Developing an awareness of your ancestral patterns can help you navigate your own life path with greater ease and confidence. And when you establish loving connections with your ancestors, it ensures that you will never walk alone.

When you open yourself to the spirits of your ancestors, you'll find that they can teach you, guide you, protect you, and help you heal. They encourage you without necessarily letting their influence be known. They listen to you and hear your call. And they deeply and empathically understand you. Those who have crossed over retain soul memories of what it was like to be human, with all its joys, heartaches, pleasures, and disappointments. They just see them from a much broader spiritual perspective.

Today, it is more important than ever that we awaken to and develop our relationship with our ancestors. At this time in our evolution, we are being called to experience our intimate connection with all beings, both visible and nonvisible. As we move through this rapid shift in human consciousness and the dramatic changes taking place on earth, we can learn from those who have walked here before us. Our forebears can help us with the ultimate restoration of balance in our relationship with our planet. They show us that we must nurture and consider the children of coming generations who will be the stewards of this return to balance. They want to help, because they are concerned about their own descendants. We need only pay them the attention they deserve and open ourselves to receiving their guidance.

I hope this book shows you not only how your ancestors can help you, but how you can help them. When our ancestors transition into the world of spirit, they can carry remnants of unhealed emotional, mental, and physical wounds they bore in life. You can help heal the echoes of these wounds so they can continue their evolution in the afterlife and find their way to the light. As you do so, you'll discover the many ways in which this impacts both you and your own descendants, so that subsequent generations never have to carry these burdens.

PART I

Understanding Ancestral Family Patterns

Chapter 1

Exploring Your Ancestry

As you begin the journey of healing your ancestral patterns, it helps to get as broad a picture as you can of what those patterns are and where they came from. You don't have to be an expert genealogist to do this. You need only reflect back on your parents and grandparents—and perhaps more distant ancestors—and gather memories, stories, and facts about their lives and personalities. Consider the historical context in which they lived and the secrets they kept. This can tell you a lot about who you are. Taking the time to contemplate your heritage can open your eyes to the unseen forces that have shaped you—forces that stretch back not just through your lifetime, but through centuries and even millennia.

In the last thirty years, there has been an explosion of research done on the ways in which our parents and early childhood experiences shape our personalities and our predisposition to both physical and mental illnesses. We've learned that adverse childhood experiences such as living through abuse, poverty, or the death of a parent can affect us for the rest of our lives. These experiences can increase our chances of suffering from anxiety, depression, addiction, and heart disease, and even predict our future educational and career achievements. Many adults go to therapy seeking to understand the ways in which their parents impacted them. In many cases, both patients and therapists assume that it is the parents who have the biggest influence on a child's life, while ignoring the many generations of ancestors standing *behind* those parents.

But in his book *The Soul's Code: In Search of Character and Calling,* Jungian psychologist James Hillman argues that the cultural belief that we are solely and uniquely shaped by our parents is a fallacy. He asserts that we are formed by forces that reach much farther back in history, and he views ancestors as a significant influence.

Without a sense of ancestors, what can we propitiate as having a direct and controlling influence over our lives, but our parents? We take literally the commandment to "Honor thy father and thy mother," which shows decency and kindness. But let's not forget that the Fifth Commandment, along with the ones preceding it, aims to eliminate all traces of pagan polytheism, to which ancestor worship is essential.

If you have strong opinions about the ways your parents and siblings shaped you as a person, the notion of looking farther back in your family tree may be new to you. Yet with just a little digging, you will find that the traits and patterns you ascribe to your parents actually have much deeper roots than you realized—sometimes stretching back hundreds of years.

Below are practices designed to help you thoroughly explore your ancestry and identify the physical, emotional, behavioral, and psychological patterns that may still be affecting you today. As you work through these exercises, you may wish to enlist the help of relatives and family friends to fill in the blanks. What does your mother remember about her aunts and uncles? What does your grandfather know about his own great-grandparents? Are there old photographs, letters, or journals available for you to study? Do online genealogical databases provide any clues?

If you don't have access to these resources, don't worry. Many of the exercises in this book can be done using nothing more than your own intuition. If you are unable to gather specific facts or memories about your blood and/or adoptive relatives, feel free to skip ahead to the next chapter. But even if you have access to only a small amount of information, it's worth gathering all that you can.

Exercise: Building a Family Tree

Gather several loose sheets of paper and draw a line down the middle of the first page. Write "Father" at the top of one side and "Mother" at the top of the other, then write down your parents' full names. Do the same on a second page, but this time write "Maternal Grandmother" and "Maternal Grandfather" and add their full names. Repeat this on the third page for your paternal grandparents, adding their full names if you know them. On the next two pages, do the same for your maternal and paternal great-grandparents.

Starting with your parents, write down any significant facts you know about them—the jobs they held, previous relationships or marriages, accidents, illnesses, and other traumas. Then add hobbies, personality traits, special skills, talents, and ambitions. Do the same for your grandparents and great-grandparents.

If you don't know much or anything at all about a certain relative, leave it blank. If you end up writing more than fits on the page, keep going for as many pages as you need. If you are adopted and know your birth parents and any previous generations, use that information to fill out these pages. If you are adopted and don't know your birth parents, create pages for them anyway, as these will serve to stimulate the connections to your biological family and its previous generations. You can complete a second family tree for your adoptive family.

Now spread the pages like an upside-down triangle on the table or floor, with the page for your parents at the bottom, topped by the ones for your grandparents, then your great-grandparents. If you want to extend this exercise by adding aunts, uncles, cousins, great-aunts, great-uncles, and so forth, go ahead. Go as far back in your ancestry as you like, adding as much information as you can. When you are done reviewing the pages, tuck them in your journal so you can refer to them as you work through other exercises.

Exercise: Identifying Ancestral Patterns

Once you've identified your ancestors and gathered as much information as you can about them, it's time to look for recurring traits and patterns.

Take four more sheets of paper. At the top of the first page, write "Physical." As you review the family tree you created in the previous exercise, do you see any notable physical traits popping up again and again? Are there common illnesses? What about injuries or accidents that can't be explained by genetics? Are the people in your ancestry physically active and athletic, or sedentary? Are they farmers who are up at the crack of dawn, or city folk who lie about in comfy beds until noon? Make a note of any patterns you see—whether positive or negative.

At the top of the second sheet, write "Emotional," then make a note of any recurring emotional traits you notice. Are your maternal aunts, great-aunts, and grandmother all known for their warmth and sweetness? Are they famous for their steely resolve? Does depression or anxiety show up frequently? Do your relatives hold grudges? Do they forgive easily? Once again, write down any patterns you see.

At the top of the third sheet, write "Behavioral," then list any traits or behaviors you identified in the previous exercise. Is your family tree peopled with sharp-witted lawyers? Courageous warriors? Intuitive artists? Do many family members suffer from addictions? If so, what types? Are there generations of divorces, teen pregnancies, or adultery? Are there priests, shamans, monks, or other contemplatives in your heritage? Make a note of any patterns you uncover.

At the top of the fourth sheet, write "Psychological," then consider which personality traits show up in your family tree. Do forgetfulness, suspicion, or optimism appear again and again? Is there a long-standing family allegiance to a certain political party? Does your family tree hold a lot of conformists, or are there some loveable oddballs in there as well? Once again, list any patterns that appear.

You now have a picture of the physical, emotional, behavioral, and psychological patterns running through your ancestral line. Keep these pages handy, and add to them as you discover more about your ancestors by working through the exercises in this book. And be sure to record your observations in your journal.

Exercise: Appreciating Historical Context

Historical events like wars, famines, economic depressions, and mass migrations can have dramatic effects that ripple down through generations. If your ancestors lived through any of these traumatic situations, you may be shaped by them as well, even if you did not personally experience them. For example, if your great-grandparents lived through a famine, you and your immediate family members may still have a fear of scarcity about food, and a strong policy of never wasting it.

For your parents, grandparents, and great-grandparents (and farther back if you are able), make a list of any significant historical events that may have shaped them. Did they live in London during World War II? Did they pick grapes during the Great Depression? Were they involved in the Civil Rights Movement? Did they immigrate from Poland to Massachusetts?

In your journal, reflect on how living through these events may have affected your ancestors and shaped their emotions, beliefs, and behaviors, and how they may have affected their physical health. Can you see any ways that these patterns are still affecting you today? If so, write them down.

Exercise: Uncovering Ancestral Wounds and Gifts

This exercise can help you identify the deepest wounds that are present in your lineage, as well as the greatest gifts. When you think back to the stories you've heard about your ancestors, do any specific traumas come to mind? Perhaps you've heard about an aunt who never laughed again after her ten-year-old son drowned in a well. Or two uncles who never spoke to each other again after having an argument on a fishing trip twenty years earlier. Conversely, do any instances of heroism, compassion, or self-sacrifice jump out at you?

Now answer the following questions, naming the ancestors in question and writing down anything you know about the incident in your journal.

- Has anyone in your ancestral line been banished or exiled from your family?

- Has anyone in your ancestral line abandoned or deserted your family?

- Has anyone in your ancestral line suffered an untimely death through suicide, murder, or recklessness?

- Has anyone in your ancestral line committed a serious crime?

- Has anyone in your ancestral line suffered from extreme scarcity?

- Has anyone in your ancestral line received a severe emotional wound?

- Has anyone in your ancestral line been either the victim or perpetrator of a colonization effort or genocide?

Now answer the following questions about gifts that may be hiding in your family tree. Once again, name the ancestors in question and write down anything you know about the incident in your journal.

- Has anyone in your ancestral line shown extreme courage or fortitude?

- Has anyone in your ancestral line shown intense love and compassion?

- Has anyone in your ancestral line made great sacrifices for others?

- Has anyone in your ancestral line overcome a big obstacle?

- Has anyone in your ancestral line been creative or clever—an artist or inventor?

- Has anyone in your ancestral line held values that are meaningful to you?

You can refer back to these lists when deciding which ancestors to work with or which ancestral patterns to address in the exercises in part II.

Exercise: Creating an Ancestral Wish List

When you think about your family and your ancestry, do you have any particular questions to which you've always wanted answers? For example, have you always longed to know why your grandfather left your grandmother? Or why everyone in your family has very vivid and prophetic dreams? Or why you can't stop thinking about certain ancestors, even though you've never met them? Maybe you've wondered if your own trajectory through life parallels that of a specific ancestor and you yearn to ask that person for guidance.

Make a list of these questions, and keep it handy as you go through the exercises in part II. Knowing *why* you are on this journey will help you stay motivated, and make the messages you receive from your ancestors easier to understand.

Chapter 2

Family Secrets

As you conduct a thorough and wide-ranging review of your family's history, you may uncover secrets. You may stumble across a revelatory journal entry or a letter, or a relative you've approached may tell you something that has thus far remained unsaid. You may even uncover secrets you've hidden from *yourself*—events that you experienced or witnessed but pushed deep down into your subconscious. In some cases, discovering these secrets can be joyful and bring about much-needed understanding. In other cases, these secrets can be painful to confront.

Due to cultural and societal prohibitions, certain facts about our families typically remain repressed, along with the strong feelings associated with them. Unfortunately, feelings like rage, lust, guilt, or fear—as well as unacceptable behaviors like incest, addictions, or eating disorders—are often expressed in some way in spite of our attempts to hold them at bay. For example, those who were molested as children may express this as sexual addiction, or those who carry a great deal of guilt may try to make others feel guilty. Even more likely, these repressed feelings and behaviors may be projected onto others in the family, who then act out these toxic influences without being aware of their original source.

A friend of mine discovered, twelve years into her marriage, that her husband was gay. She was shocked and distraught, and it took some time to reconcile herself with this knowledge, because she claimed that she'd had no clue. Several years later, her daughter revealed that she was in love with another woman. "When I found out," she said, "it brought up all the old feelings about my ex-husband and his announcing that he was gay. I thought I had coped with it, but it was a double shocker to hear that my daughter was as well."

My friend went on to tell me that after a rocky few months, she was able to accept her daughter's relationship. Indeed, she celebrates the fact that her daughter lives in a world in which she doesn't have to hide her sexual orientation—unlike her husband, who was born a generation before. When she contemplates her own descendants, she is happy to know that this pattern of hiding and secrecy is starting to heal.

Who Am I?

Sometimes family secrets are so huge that discovering the truth behind them turns a person's life around 180 degrees. An Australian friend of mine discovered a life-changing family secret when he was sixteen years old and in juvenile detention, careening down a course that had a seemingly inevitable outcome. He had olive skin and dark, penetrating eyes. "I didn't know who I was," he told me. "I wasn't sure if I was Filipino, Mexican, Samoan—I had no solid identity. I never knew my father, and my mother was completely Anglo—mostly Irish, I think."

Then he described a day that he would always remember—the day his paternal grandfather showed up to take him out of detention. His grandfather was Aboriginal. He signed my friend out and took him to the land of his ancestors in northern Queensland, where he stayed for two years exploring the ways of his people. He learned their language, their sacred songs and dances, and how to play the didgeridoo. It took a while for him to integrate the truth about his identity, which had been kept under wraps for his entire life.

Eventually, my friend visited his father, who was in jail, and learned another shocking family secret. He had been conceived when his father raped his mother. As he struggled to come to grips with this knowledge, he realized that he didn't feel angry toward his father. Instead, he felt compassion for him. Not pity, but compassion. This was his father—the good, the bad, and the ugly. His father told him that he was proud of him and of the work he was doing for their people.

When he got up to leave, my friend had the strong feeling that this would be the last time he would ever see his father—some impression he couldn't pinpoint. The feeling was so strong that he considered asking the guards to put a watch on him, but decided that would violate a confidence. Yet he somehow sensed that his father wanted to die. Now that he had seen how the son he had never known had become a man, his work on this planet was finished. The next day, he got the news that his father had hanged himself. He had crossed over, and was now truly an ancestor.

I have no doubt that this father and those ancestors who had crossed into the afterlife before him received the benefit of my friend's healing journey. The revelation of this potent family secret started him down the path of healing and altered not only his own ancestral patterns, but those of his entire people. From that point on, he made choices that eventually led him to become a key advocate for Aboriginal youth.

Four Degrees of Family Secrets

John Bradshaw is the author of several excellent books that offer insights into healing wounds that result from growing up in a dysfunctional family. In *Family Secrets,* he outlines four degrees of toxicity that derive from family secrets: victimization, demoralization, violation of trust, and shaming.

The first degree, and the most toxic, results from secrets that are deadly and involve victimization—criminal activities like murder, assault, and torture, as well as sexual crimes like rape, incest, and sexual abuse.

The second degree stems from actions that are demoralizing and potentially dangerous, though not necessarily lethal. This includes behaviors like substance abuse, eating disorders, addictions to sex or love or gambling, and identity issues based in adoption or questionable paternity. While it's ultimately best that this type of secret be confronted and disclosed, he warns, doing so can involve some backlash for the one keeping the secret, as well as for the person confronting the secret-keeper.

The third degree of toxicity derives from actions or circumstances that can be damaging because they can violate a person's freedom and/or boundaries. Although less damaging than the first two degrees, these secrets create distrust and close off communication. And when disclosed, they can put the subject of the secret—as well as the person disclosing it—at some emotional risk. According to Bradshaw, these secrets include family enmeshments in which roles are unclear and boundaries are crossed, marital secrets like closeted gay/lesbian marriage, infidelity, hidden resentments, emotional and mental illness, and denial of death or illness.

The fourth degree of toxicity is the least harmful, but nonetheless distressful. The disclosure of these secrets most often puts the one keeping them at emotional risk. This category includes feelings of toxic shame—guilt, fear, anxiety, and depression—as well as cultural shame, which can include body issues, social awkwardness, and spiritual or religious crisis.

When these family secrets remain buried, they end up being projected onto others or passed along through the generations. Their toxic influence can remain in the lineage for several generations, often being acted out by one or more family members until active healing takes place.

Often, it's only when a descendant begins the journey of healing these ancestral patterns—as my friend did—that these secrets come out. Bringing them out into the open creates an opportunity to release their hold on family members, and frees subsequent generations to go through life without being burdened by them.

Exercise: Revealing Family Secrets

In the course of your research and reflections on your ancestry, have you uncovered any family secrets? Are they happy secrets or sad ones? Where do they fall on the scale from most to least toxic? Which patterns have been perpetuated through your family tree as a result of them?

Make a list of any family secrets you have uncovered and note their effects in your journal. In part II, we will look at ways to communicate with the ancestors who were involved in them in order to facilitate healing, even if they crossed over long ago.

Exercise: Practicing Self-Reflection

Now that you have conducted an extensive review of your family tree, including any secrets you may have found there, make a list of the patterns you would most like to heal. Remember that by healing these patterns in yourself, you are also healing them for your ancestors, as well as for generations to come.

Here is an example for each category of traits we discussed in the Introduction:

- *Physical*: Heal a pattern of sedentary living and preventable illnesses.

- *Emotional*: Heal a pattern of holding grudges and reconcile with an estranged sister.

- *Behavioral*: Heal a pattern of overspending and financial insecurity.

- *Psychological*: Heal a pattern of chronic fear, suspicion, and secrecy.

Keep this list handy as you work through the rest of the exercises in this book.

Chapter 3

The Dark Law

While completing the exercises in the previous two chapters, you may have stumbled across what I call the "dark law"—an unwritten rule that you have learned to obey and that has shaped your life in dramatic ways. Your dark law, whatever that may be, was typically born out of a traumatic experience you had in early childhood that caused you to form an entrenched and largely unconscious belief about yourself. In turn, you related to your environment and developed your emerging personality based on that belief, without being fully aware of it.

Your dark law is often the result of ancestral patterns, with one or more of your most immediate ancestors being shaped by a similar imperative. For example, if your family lost its home to foreclosure when you were a child, your dark law may be something along the lines of: "There is no shelter in this world." When you look into your ancestry, you may find that your great-great-grandparents were tenant farmers who were forced off their land—and that "your" dark law actually goes back much farther than you. The good news is that you can discover what your law is and do work to counteract it, breaking the spell not only for yourself, but for future generations.

Below are a few examples of dark laws and ways to counteract them. Any of these may form the basis of your own negativity and lack of self-worth. That is why becoming aware of them is so crucial. Recognizing and acknowledging these ingrained beliefs can prompt you to rethink and reevaluate conclusions you reached when you were in your earliest formative years and promote active healing.

> *No one will ever love me because I'm bad.* This core belief comes from constant criticism, degradation, and emotional abuse from a significant adult. I recall seeing a billboard years ago that said: "Words can hurt." In fact, they can sometimes hurt even more than physical abuse—especially at a young and tender age, when you're more vulnerable to their lasting effects. This dark law can indicate that you

have an ancestral pattern of parents speaking harshly to children. Perhaps your grandparents spoke this way to your parents and your great-grandparents spoke that way to them, resulting in generations of family members who don't consider themselves worthy of love. You can work to release this dark law by deciding to love yourself and speaking kindly to yourself, while offering the same gift to your own children and grandchildren.

People can never be trusted. This dark law may arise when an adult to whom you look for your very survival betrays your trust time and again. This can lead to social awkwardness, difficulties with relationships, loneliness, and isolation. Do your relatives show patterns of suspicion and avoidance? Did one or both of your parents counsel you to always rely on yourself, because you can never be sure that anyone else will show up for you? If you stumble across significant instances of betrayal as you take stock of your family tree, this dark law may be operating in your ancestry. You can work to release it by paying attention to the ways in which people in your life *have* been trustworthy and reliable.

I will be abandoned and left alone to fend for myself in the world. If your mother, father, or other caregiver abandoned you at a young age, you may expect to be abandoned, or you may abandon others as a self-protective mechanism. Abandonment can also take "milder" forms, like being shipped off to boarding school, sent to live with relatives, or simply left alone to grapple with problems that were too big for you to handle without the help of caring adults. Does your family tree reveal instances of abandonment? Do your relatives show extreme self-sufficiency or even a fear of relying too much on others? Do your family members have difficulty making lifelong commitments to others, and honoring them? If so, fear of abandonment may be your dark law. You can work to release it by paying attention to the ways in which you are now competent and able to navigate the world as an adult, and by doing healing practices that involve the ancestors who abandoned you.

Life is not worth living. Hope is a quality that helps you through dark periods in your life. If an early trauma leaves you feeling hopeless and powerless, it can lead to chronic depression, suicidal thoughts, or self-harm behaviors. If suffering was your primary experience as a young child, it can lead you to conclude that it's just not worth the effort to continue. One of my clients recalls her mother telling her repeatedly that she wished she'd never been born. It's easy to see how she harbored this dark law as a result. If you have many relatives who were forced to confront hopeless situations like wars, famines, or concentration camps, or relatives who were severely abused by their parents or caregivers, these ancestral patterns may be in urgent need of healing. Releasing this dark law may require extensive grieving, as well as intentionally seeking out moments of love, joy, and connection with others.

My Dark Law

My own dark law is: "I don't want to be a problem." Its corollary is: "I don't really have any effect on others." In my efforts to avoid being a problem, I tend to hide those aspects of myself about which I feel shame. As a child, I was quiet and shy. I always thought of myself as a weird kid, different from others in my family, as well as from classmates and friends. But I now understand my obsessive-compulsive nature and the addictions in which I indulged as a young man—like smoking up to two packs of cigarettes a day. These were simply a means of trying to medicate the demons inside me instead of facing them.

Over the years, I uncovered and healed my wounds by continually seeking answers through psychotherapy, group therapy, and workshops. Eventually, I discovered my spiritual path through shamanism. Through my ancestral healing work, I realized that the same dark law that was affecting me was woven throughout my family tree, with my own father and grandfather exhibiting many of the same traits. This realization was critical, as it helped me understand that this law wasn't unique to me. It was a pattern with a long history that had affected many who came before me. Knowing this, I felt even more inspired to heal.

Although it's still lurking in the shadows just on the edge of my vision, this crusty old dark law no longer rules me. I accept that some people may see me as a problem in certain moments, but I no longer allow myself to see that as a burden. Moreover, I realize that, through my writings, workshops, and healing sessions, I have affected the lives of thousands of others. This isn't ego talking; it's an acceptance that flies in the face of this formerly entrenched belief and the world I had constructed to prove that my dark law was correct. Because I have healed this destructive trait in myself, I know that future generations of my family will be less likely to feel its presence in their own lives.

The next three exercises can help you identify and release your own dark law.

Exercise: Discovering Your Dark Law

You can discover your own dark law by writing down your answers to each of these questions:

- Do you resonate with any of the examples listed above? If so, which one(s)?

- Do you recall any early traumatic experiences that may have led to a self-defeating core belief? Describe these experiences and any conclusions about life you drew from them.

- Ask one or two of your closest friends or family members about any self-sabotaging behav-

iors they see in you. Their answers may give
you clues as to the nature of your dark law.

Once you have an idea of what your dark law is,
write it out on a page in your journal. Over the next
three weeks, simply observe your thoughts, feelings,
and behaviors as they relate to this core negative belief.
How has this belief shaped your life? Who would you
be without it?

Exercise: Creating Healing Affirmations

One particularly effective technique for confronting
and deconstructing a dark law is the use of affirmations that directly contradict that negative belief. For
instance, my belief that "I have no effect on others"
can be contradicted by the statement: "I, Steven, have a
powerful effect on others." Or: "I, Steven, have a strong
presence with others." Another affirmation I've worked
with effectively in the past is: "I, Steven, am a powerful
and loving man." By repeating these affirmations day
after day, I slowly eroded my dark law and drained it
of its power.

Here are some tips for creating effective affirmations that can help you release your dark law:

- Compose one or two statements that contradict the core negative belief. For example, if your dark law is "It's not worth trying," craft a statement like: "My efforts always pay off."

- Always insert your name into your affirmations. For example: "I, _____(your name), _____(statement)."

- Once you have settled on an affirmation, repeat it ten to twelve times, twice each day.

- Pause after each repetition and notice any thoughts, feelings, or behaviors that arise in reaction to it. If it's an effective affirmation, you will sense a reaction to it. Just observe this without shame or judgment, take a breath, and repeat the affirmation again.

Repeat this process every day for twenty-one days and watch what happens. It can take you a significant step forward toward releasing your dark law. Be sure to record your observations in your journal.

Exercise: Changing Your Filter

A dark law causes you to view the world through a filter, seeing only what it allows you to see. For example, if your negative belief concerns abandonment, you may selectively pay attention to instances in which the people in your life seem to let you down, while ignoring all the ways they show up for you. If it concerns the futility of trying, you may spend hours ruminating about all the times your efforts were in vain, while ignoring all the times your hard work paid off. To combat this tendency, try changing the filter through which you see the world.

Start by writing down your dark law as a statement—for instance: "All my efforts are in vain." Then make a list of all the times this statement wasn't true. For example, there was a probably a time when you studied for a test and got a good grade. Or perhaps you managed to fix your car after hours of tinkering, or won over a grumpy neighbor with acts of kindness and generosity.

Add to this list any time you notice an aspect of your life that counteracts your dark law, and record your impressions in your journal.

Chapter 4

Rewriting Ancestral Stories

In my book *Sacred Ceremony*, I recounted the tale of how when my mother died, my father took her ashes back to our hometown. When he returned, he stuck around for about a year and gave away a lot of his possesions. Then he drove back to our hometown with what he had left and died three weeks later—of a broken heart, I'm sure, although something else was listed on the death certificate.

Three years after his death, I went to my father's grave and had a conversation with him. Actually, it was kind of a one-sided conversation, as I called to his spirit and then simply listened. It was the first time I'd attempted to make contact with either of my parents since their deaths. Sitting by his grave with tears pricking at the corners of my eyes, I felt a strong sense of his presence.

My father was a quiet man—sensitive on the inside, but with a gruff exterior that came in part from working construction his whole life and driving heavy machines like bulldozers. He was also an alcoholic. Often, when he came home from the local bar, my mother railed at him about his drinking. Dad got belligerent; Mom got mad. And the fighting ensued from there. They loved each other deeply, but this was a side of their marriage that was destructive for all.

For many years after I left home, I convinced myself that my stepbrothers and stepsister didn't think much of my father—their stepfather. I assumed that they most likely felt as if he had intruded into their lives and resented his excessive drinking. I assumed that they disliked him intensely and blamed him for the fights and the misery that occurred as a result. At least, this was the story I had written about their feelings toward him.

Then, at a family gathering that took place shortly before I visited my father's grave, I decided to poll my siblings to see how they felt about my dad. I first approached my sister and asked her about her feelings, saying: "I bet you really thought he was a tyrant." Her immediate reply rocked me back on my heels. "Oh, no!" she said. "He was a good man—a saint to put up with our mother all those years." As we continued to talk about her memories, it became apparent that she carried some deep wounds from her relationship with our mother, but spoke highly of my dad.

Next, I asked my older brother what he thought and got a similar response—my father had been very good to them. My younger brother agreed that he had taken good care of us all and was a hardworking man.

After speaking with my siblings, I had to completely revise the story I'd been telling myself for so many years. The more I questioned the conclusions I had drawn, the more I came to appreciate my father for how he had married a woman with three children and taken them in as his own. I recalled him telling me more than once that he tried to treat all four of us equally, even though I was his only biological offspring. And then I realized that I was playing out that ancestral pattern in my own life. I had also married a woman with two children by a different father!

As I sat at my father's grave, I was able to truly hear and experience him, instead of the story about him I had been carrying around. I felt a sense of gratitude for his positive qualities that had eluded me when I'd focused only on the difficult aspects of his personality. Most important, I got a sense of him as a whole person—someone who had taken both positive and negative actions in his lifetime.

Appreciating Positive Traits

We all tell ourselves stories about our parents, grandparents, and other relatives. "My mom was high-strung and controlling." "My grandfather never said I love you to anyone." Over time, we begin to mistake these stories for the whole truth of who those people are or were. We focus on the dark law and the ways it shaped our family line. Yet the flip side of identifying your family's dark law is appreciating the good qualities in your ancestors that you may have overlooked, minimized, or undervalued, and seeing their actions in context.

For example, maybe your mother *was* high-strung, but only because she was constantly trying to protect herself and her children from an abusive partner. Take a moment to consider the many ways in which you benefited from her vigilance, rather than thinking only about the ways her negative qualities caused you harm. Maybe your grandfather never said "I love you," but remember that he worked in a coal mine every day so that his children could go to school, and brought his paycheck home to the family instead of drinking it away with other miners at a bar.

Often, the very people we cast in our minds as villains have made enormous sacrifices that go unnoticed. This is not to say that good deeds and sacrifices excuse bad behavior like abuse. But when you take a little time to appreciate your ancestors' positive traits, you can come to understand them better and see them with greater compassion. Ever since my conversation with my siblings, every time I make contact with either one of my parents, the experience is healing—both for them and for myself.

By seeking out and honoring your ancestors' positive qualities, you can make the stories you tell about them more nuanced. This can help heal their legacy in your own life. The next four exercises give you an opportunity to rewrite the stories you tell about those who have crossed over, and carry that new storyline forward into generations to come.

Exercise: Exposing Your Headlines

When people ask you about your family, what are the "headlines" you use to summarize each parent or relative's character? For example: "My mom was a workaholic" or, "My sister always hated me" or, "My dad escaped into la-la land every chance he got."

Find a photograph of your parents, siblings, and any other relatives or ancestors you want to work with. As you gaze at each one, think of your headline for that person and hold it in your mind. Notice any emotions and physical sensations that come up as you look at this person through the lens you've chosen.

When you have gone through the entire series of photos, start over at the beginning. This time, pretend that you are looking at pictures of strangers—people you've never seen before. How do your emotions and physical sensations change when you look at the photos this time? Does your posture soften? Do you feel curiosity rather than judgment? Do memories come up that contradict your original headline? Can you see glimmers of positive traits in these people that you couldn't see before? Record your impressions in your journal.

Exercise: Gathering New Perspectives

My headlines for my father changed dramatically after I asked my siblings to share their memories and opinions with me. Their responses gave me a whole new perspective on him. This exercise can help you change the filter through which you see a relative or ancestor for whom you have written a negative or mostly negative headline, and develop a new story that includes their positive traits.

Start by making a list of people you can ask about your relative—siblings, aunts and uncles, old neighbors, coworkers, former partners, teachers, or anyone else who knew the person well or had significant interactions with them. Then contact these people and ask if they would be willing to share their memories and give you insight into your relative's life and personality. These conversations can take place in person, over the phone, by video chat, or even by email.

What do you learn from these new perspectives? Does some of the information you receive contradict your headline about that person, or does it mostly confirm it? Do you learn things you might not have found out in any other way? Do you understand your relative's behavior a little better, even if you still don't agree with it? Jot down your thoughts in your journal.

Exercise: Revising Your Headlines

The stories we tell about ourselves and our ancestors are like magic spells. They encourage certain truths to flourish and persist, while discouraging others. But once you have identified the headlines you use to describe relatives and gathered new perspectives on them, you can write new headlines and revise the stories you tell about them.

Write down your old headline for each relative you are working with. Then write a new headline that reflects the new perspectives you've gathered. For example: "My father was an alcoholic, but he was an extremely loyal man who tried hard to be fair," or "My mom struggled to be warm and nurturing, but she showed up for us in ways we didn't always appreciate or recognize."

The next time a new acquaintance asks you about your family, make a point of sharing this revised headline. How does it feel to speak about your parents and/or ancestors in a new way? Reflect on those feelings in your journal.

Exercise: Writing Future Headlines

This exercise encourages you to contemplate the headlines that your family members and descendants will someday write about you. When you imagine your children, nieces and nephews, and grandchildren telling friends about you, what do you think they will say? Write down any phrases or sentences that come to mind.

How do you feel when you look at this list? Do you feel a pang of sadness or regret, or a flush of pride and satisfaction? Is there anything about this list you would like to change?

Now write down your ideal headlines—the things you *want* people to say about you after you're gone, or even while you're still on earth. For example: "She was never too busy to be kind," or "He always put truth and justice above personal gain."

Choose the headline that you most want to have as your legacy. Write it on a small card and pin it in a place where you will see it often, or carry it in your pocket and look at it frequently. Remember that, as long as you are alive, it is never too late to write a new headline for yourself.

Chapter 5

Messages from Your Ancestors

In part II of this book, I introduce you to a wide range of practices for interacting with your ancestors, no matter how long ago they departed from this earth. But in order for you to get the most out of these practices, you must learn about the messages we receive from our ancestors and the many forms they can take.

When you think of spirit messages, you may think of rare and dramatic events like God handing the tablets to Moses. But the truth is that messages from spirits are much more common and ordinary than many of us have been led to believe. Many who have suffered a personal loss feel as if the appearance of a certain bird, or a butterfly, or a rainbow can indicate that the spirit of their loved one is nearby. For them, these elements of the natural world are spirit messages. Hearing a certain song on the radio can also be a spirit message if the song has significance for you. So can glimpsing an advertisement, or receiving an email with a certain subject line, or having a short conversation with a stranger. What makes something a spirit message is its personal relevance—the relation it has to a question that's been on your mind, or an answer you've been seeking.

The more you open yourself to receiving these messages, the more you will realize that they are all around you, all the time. The universe is always speaking to you through myriad channels. Your ancestors may use whatever channel they have at their disposal to communicate with you, whether that's through dreams, visions, symbols, coincidences, or instances of seeming "luck." Depending on your unique proclivities, you may tune in to one channel more easily than others, or you may receive messages through a variety of channels.

Tuning In

There are essentially four channels through which we receive information from both the physical world and the world of spirit—clairvoyance (clear seeing), clairaudience (clear hearing), clairsentience (clear sensing), and claircognizance (clear thought). When you attempt to contact your ancestors across space and time, you quickly realize that you receive messages through some of these channels more easily than others. For example, some people are very good at visualizing and tend to receive spirit messages in the form of visions or images, while others are gifted at metaphor and tend to receive them in the form of symbols or signs.

Most people tend to tune in primarily to one or two of these channels, while using the others only rarely or not at all. Since you'll be working with ancestors through the medium of your usual senses, it's best to communicate with them in the way that is most comfortable and natural for you. Let's take a closer look at each of these channels.

Clairvoyance

Clairvoyance is the ability to see things clearly. When you close your eyes, are you able to conjure up images easily? If so, you may be more likely to receive visual messages. Ancestors may appear to you more vividly than they do to others. People who are more visual often report seeing apparitions like very light holographic images. As you look at a photo of your grandfather, you may perceive a faint image of him just to the side of the picture. He may make some sort of gesture in an attempt to communicate with you. For instance, he may point to a photo of your daughter and, when you direct your attention to it, he may smile, as if to say, "I'm watching out for her."

If the visual channel is one of your strongest, you may also be more likely to get messages in the form of recurring images you see in your environment. For example, imagine you've been considering a pilgrimage to Mount Shasta in Northern California because you've heard so much about it being very special and sacred. As you're thinking about it, you spot a Shasta Cola on the supermarket shelf. Later that same day, you and a friend visit a bookstore and there's a poster with Mount Shasta on it. Then you go to dinner and there's a painting of a mountain on the wall and your friend comments that it looks like Mount Shasta. If you are tuned in to spirit messages, you'll know it's time to pack your bags and get ready for your pilgrimage!

Clairaudience

Clairaudience is the ability to hear things clearly. If you are a person with a well-developed sense of hearing and strong listening skills, you may get spirit messages in the form of words spoken by your inner voice—what I sometimes call "whispers in my ear." For example, while clearing out your great-grandmother's house after her passing, you may hear a voice telling you to look under the bed, only to find a box of letters hidden there.

As with the visual channel, you may also receive auditory messages through sounds and conversations in your external environment. For instance, let's say I receive an email from someone I know in Australia. Then while I'm at the mall, I overhear someone talking about Australia. Later that day, I turn on the radio and hear a song played by an Australian band. Although I may not be entirely sure what these messages mean, that's enough of a pattern to make me pay closer attention. So I start to ask myself: Am I supposed to go to Australia? Or write about Australia? Or contact someone I know there? The meaning will become clear as I listen for more signs.

Clairsentience

Clairsentience is the ability to sense things clearly. When you perceive information from spirits in this way, you become aware of sensations in your body and any corresponding emotions that arise. People who receive spirit messages in this way describe it as getting a *feeling* about something. These feelings indicate that something is going on at the instinctual level, a kind of physical resonance or vibrational congruency with the messages your ancestors are trying to communicate.

Clairsentient messages can take the form of sensations or emotions, or a combination of the two. You may sense an aroma that has no apparent source in your physical environment—perhaps a fragrance that your grandmother used to wear indicating that she is near. Images may follow, or you may hear something in your inner voice triggered by this ancestor's presence. Or you may just get a strong feeling about something. For example, when I get a sense of my brother's spirit, I experience feelings of joy and sadness as tears well up and a smile comes to my face. If I detect the odor of cigarette smoke although nobody nearby is smoking, this tells me that my brother, who was a lifelong smoker, is with me.

This is how the vast majority of people perceive spirit messages. My sister recently lost her husband after a long illness. Although she doesn't typically delve into the psychic realm, about a year after he died I asked her if she ever thought he was still around in some way. Without hesitating, she said, "Oh, yeah!" Then I asked her how she knew. Did she see him? Hear him? Feel him? Or just know he was with her? And she replied, "I can feel him here."

Claircognizance

"I don't know how I knew—I just *knew*." This is a common statement from those whose main channel for receiving spirit messages is claircognizance—sometimes called inspiration, intuition, or insight. People who are more analytical are more likely to receive messages from spirits in this way.

Sometimes, significant revelations can occur during meditation—for instance, finding a creative resolution for an ancestral pattern you've been trying to unwind. I think of this as downloading information and messages from the ancestors. When this occurs, it isn't always evident that your ancestors are the source. In fact, we often attribute these insights to our own brilliance!

Atmospheric Interference

There are four conditions that can interfere with your ability to receive spirit messages, either by blocking them or distorting them. This kind of "atmospheric interference" can make it more difficult to discern whether these messages are coming from your ancestors or are being generated by your own ego. These four conditions are grief, pain, self-pity, and anger and blame. If you are dealing with one or more of these conditions, don't worry. We all struggle with them from time to time. But becoming aware of them can help you recognize them sooner and take steps to release them gently. Let's take a look at the effects each one of these conditions can have, and how you can keep your channels free of interference so that spirit messages can come through.

Grief

Losing someone or something special to you usually triggers the very human process of grief—a natural response to loss. When you're in the depths of the grieving process, you can more easily forget your relationship with the spirit world, or even deny that relationship because you're feeling hurt and abandoned. If your mind is occupied with the denial, anger, bargaining, or sadness stages of grief, you may experience a fogginess and lack of clarity that makes it challenging to perceive spirit messages. But remaining open to these messages despite this interference—and especially to the support and guidance coming through from your ancestors—can help you navigate your passage through this difficult time. It takes work and intentionality to get back to this state of openness, however.

Pain

When it hurts, it hurts. And the more intense the pain, the more it hurts. It doesn't matter whether it's physical, emotional, or mental pain; they all blend together anyway. Pain can suck up all of your attention and energy, making it nearly impossible for you to receive the spirit messages that are coming through for you.

The first step in counteracting this type of interference is to take whatever reasonable actions are available to alleviate your pain—massage, yoga, exercise, therapy, medication, or some form of medical treatment. Once you have done what you can to alleviate your pain in a healthy way, simply make a conscious decision to remain open to spirit messages, even as you experience the pain. Try using an affirmation like: "Even though I am feeling pain, I remain open to receiving messages from the Divine," or "Even as I experience this pain, I know that my ancestors are guiding and supporting me."

Self-Pity

Self-pity, like grief, can feel all-consuming. When you experience self-pity, your mind may be filled with stories about how you've been hurt or wronged. You may ruminate endlessly about the ways in which life is unfair, while overlooking the many gifts and blessings flowing your way.

Once, I was lagging behind in a very intense exercise class. I confess I had begun to feel sorry for myself, then I heard the coach say: "You volunteered for this, Farmer!" And I realized that he was right. It changed my whole outlook and my whole workout. "You volunteered for this!" is ultimately a good reminder that, from your soul's perspective, you made a choice to incarnate into this family in this lifetime, and part of the deal is going through these kinds of soul lessons and addressing your ancestral patterns. You can work through this type of interference by simply affirming that you *chose* to be here and are willing to learn.

Anger and Blame

It's very human to feel angry in reaction to an unexpected hurt or disappointment. How you deal with that anger is heavily influenced by your ancestral patterns. Holding on to the energy of anger, and especially of blame, can completely block any connection to the world of spirit, and certainly interfere with any communication with your ancestors.

Blame is related to self-pity in that it keeps you focused on what *shouldn't* have happened, instead of on what you want to create in your life. When you are angrily blaming others for the wrongs they have done, you are in a closed-down state in which you are unlikely to hear the whispers of your ancestors, and unable to feel curiosity, wonder, or reverence. You can counteract this kind of interference by using an affirmation like: "Even though I'm not happy about the things so-and-so did, I trust that the universe has a plan for that person just as it does for me," or "I trust that unexpected blessings are flowing toward me, even as I feel hurt or disappointed by this temporary turn of events."

Statements like these can bring you back into an open and curious mindset in which you can more easily perceive spirit messages. The next two exercises can help as well.

Exercise: Finding Your Channel

This exercise will help you detect your strongest perceptual channel for receiving spirit messages—seeing, hearing, sensing, or intuition. For most of us, our predominant modality for perceiving the everyday world is very likely to be the primary way in which we connect with the spirit world.

For the next several days, simply observe how you make the simplest of choices in ordinary reality. What are the most important considerations about where you live? How do you shop for things? How do you decide what to wear? Are visual considerations at the top of your list, or do you pay more attention to sound? Do you rely on a "feeling" to make your choice, or do you analyze situations and think them over?

If you're still not sure, consider how you respond when someone asks you a question. If you look up or straight ahead as you answer, you're more visually oriented. If you look to either side, you're more likely to use your hearing to perceive messages. If you look down, you're more likely to take in information through your body and your senses.

These aren't hard-and-fast rules. You may find that you can take in information in any or all of these ways. And certainly, the more you practice paying attention to potential messages from your ancestors, the more flexible your capacity to tune in to these messages will become.

Exercise: Resolving Interference

This practice will help you gently resolve the conditions that may be interfering with your ability to tune in to spirit messages, whether those conditions take the form of grief, pain, self-pity, or anger and blame.

First, identify which of the four conditions you are experiencing. Next, recall that your ancestors also experienced grief, pain, self-pity, and anger from time to time. Allow yourself to feel deeply down your lineage, noticing how these universal human experiences are present in your ancestors' lives. Allow yourself to feel compassion for ancestors who suffered just as you are suffering now.

Say: "May the skill and compassion with which I hold this suffering travel back down my family lineage to heal my ancestors," then imagine that you are literally holding your suffering in your arms, taking good care of it and helping it heal. Know that the work you are doing is benefiting both your ancestors and generations yet to come.

PART II

Healing Ancestral Family Patterns

Chapter 6

Channeling Forgiveness

One of the most powerful healings we can experience takes place when we forgive an ancestor for hurting us in some way. As long as we carry anger, hurt, fear, or vindictiveness toward an ancestor, we are living with a "soul poison" that can have insidious effects—not only on us, but also on others in our lives. Truly forgiving someone is a tremendous release that opens the door to a previously unknown state of freedom. Forgiving our ancestors also frees them to continue their journey in the afterlife.

Because many of us are drawn to ancestral healing work out of a desire to forgive someone who has hurt us, it can come as a surprise to learn that we often have to forgive ourselves before we can truly forgive others. In fact, the whole concept of forgiving ourselves may feel counterintuitive, or even offensive. "Forgive myself for what?" we may ask. Yet many of us carry self-blame for the wrongs that were done to us. On some level, we still believe it's our fault that we were shamed, or punished, or abused in various ways, even when we know, on an intellectual level, that this cannot possibly be true.

As children, we assume that adults know what they're doing—especially those adults who are charged with taking care of us. So when parents, grandparents, or other adults mistreat children in some way, they inevitably assume it's their fault. As they grow, this assumption gets buried under fear, hurt, and anger, so that, as adults, they may not be consciously aware of feelings of self-blame. Instead, those feelings get acted out through polarized behavior patterns, like being overly aggressive or overly passive in dealing with life.

Sexual abuse can be especially confusing, because we're inherently sexual and sensual beings wired to experience pleasurable sensations when our bodies are touched in certain ways. If you were touched in a sexual way as a child, you may have felt confusion and fear, but you may also have felt pleasurable sensations that you buried deep under the surface. You may feel ashamed and guilty about having "enjoyed" the experience, which only adds to the sense that it was somehow your fault.

Before attempting to forgive an ancestor who abused you, always check to see if you are carrying self-blame for any aspect of that experience, and forgive yourself for that first. This will pave the way to being able to forgive your ancestor in an authentic way, rather than forcing yourself toward a sense of forgiveness for which you aren't ready.

True forgiveness cannot be rushed. If you're not ready to forgive—either yourself or others—don't push yourself. Trust your process and move forward only if and when it feels right to do so. The exercises that follow can help you explore the process of forgiveness from the point of view of both yourself *and* your ancestors. If any of these practices feel too intense, it is perfectly fine to leave them for another time.

Exercise: Forgiving Yourself

Self-forgiveness is an essential part of ancestral healing. This exercise can help you identify any feelings of shame or guilt you may feel about traumatic events in your past and reconcile you with those responsible for them.

For a few minutes each day, stand straight and tall in front of a full-length mirror. As you look at your image in the mirror, notice any emotions or physical sensations that arise. Scan your body up and down a couple of times, and continue observing how you feel. Be sure to breathe steadily and easily. Notice if you tense up or if your breathing falters. If this happens, remind yourself to relax. Notice any memories that are triggered when you look at your own reflection.

Call in any protection you may want—spirit guides or ancestors with whom you have a loving relationship. Ask them to maintain a boundary of golden light around you so you feel safe. Trust that they will take good care of you. Then call any ancestors who mistreated you and ask them to sit at a safe distance—as far away as necessary to make you feel safe, but still within your view, even if that means they appear as a tiny speck.

Make eye contact with your reflection and fix your gaze on your own eyes. State out loud to your reflection: "I forgive you. It was not your fault." Pause and notice what your mind and body do after making this statement. Do you feel awkward? Uncertain? Do you laugh or fidget? Do you cry or collapse? Let your body make any posture adjustments or movements it needs to. When you allow your body to react, you purge those old feelings of guilt and shame, and let go of any judgments you have made based on them.

Repeat your forgiveness statement ten to twelve times, pausing each time to witness your reaction. When you feel complete, thank the ancestors you called in, and close the ritual with any gesture that feels meaningful to you—bowing, rattling, or clapping your hands. Record your experience in your journal.

Exercise: Ancestral Dialogue

Once you have forgiven yourself and released any feelings of guilt or shame surrounding events in your past, you can offer forgiveness to those responsible for hurting you. Set two chairs facing each other at a comfortable distance. Sit in one of the chairs, then close your eyes and take three deep breaths as you call in any protective spirits or loving ancestors you want to have with you during the exercise.

Invite the ancestor you want to forgive to sit in the chair opposite you and feel, see, hear, or simply sense their presence. When your ancestor is present, share how you feel about what they did. Ask any questions you may have. Say whatever you want, but say it in three to five minutes.

When you are done, stand up, take three deep breaths, and then slowly walk over to the other chair. Ask the ancestor if you can merge so you can both heal, and so your descendants can heal as well. If the answer is "yes," gently sit in the chair and close your eyes.

Assume the posture of your ancestor. What are this person's fears? What about joys? Is there sadness? Grief? Hurt? How does your body feel as you tune in to this presence? What is it like to have this spirit with you or next to you? Is it uncomfortable? If merging with your ancestor feels too intense, you can place a third chair close by and sit there instead.

How does "ancestor you" perceive "physical you"? Are they happy to see you? Do they feel shame? What does this person want you to know or understand? Speaking as your ancestor, address your physical self, conveying whatever comes through. At the end of three to five minutes, stand up again and break away from your ancestor's energy, leaving them sitting in the chair.

Return to your own chair and tell your ancestor how you feel. Don't hold back. Do you feel angry? Hurt? Fearful? Loved? Respected? Speak to them as if they were actually in that chair—across time and space. Speak freely, knowing the ancestor must listen, then switch chairs again. When you are once again merged, allow the ancestor to respond.

Continue this dialogue, switching places as many times as you wish. Clear the energy you carried in either role before moving from one chair to the other. Always pause between each exchange, then take three breaths and move to the opposite chair.

Eventually, each chair will become anchored with the energy of the role you're in. When your dialogue feels complete, release the ancestor, thank your helping spirits, and take a few minutes to journal about what this experience was like for you.

Exercise: Passing On Forgiveness

A friend and colleague of mine shared the following forgiveness exercise with me in a personal interview.

Begin by thinking of an ancestor you have held a grudge against or judged, or one you simply didn't like very much. As in the previous exercise, place two chairs facing each other at a comfortable distance—one for you and one for your ancestor. When you are ready, close your eyes and take three slow, deep breaths. Let your body relax as much as possible.

Recall a time when you felt forgiveness for someone—a moment when you shifted from feeling angry, hurt, vindictive, or hateful to feeling compassionate and possibly even loving toward someone who had wounded you. Find that place of forgiveness in your heart and mind, and especially in your body. Once you have found it, stand up, go to the other chair and offer this forgiveness to your ancestor in some way—perhaps by speaking a few words, making a gesture, or communicating with them through feeling.

Sit in your ancestor's chair and allow yourself to merge with their energy. Notice how they feel after being forgiven. What do they want to say to you? What has changed in your ancestor's body and mind?

You can choose to stop here, or continue the dialogue for as long as you wish. If you continue, it's important to keep switching chairs so that you don't mix your own energy with that of your ancestor.

Chapter 7

Healing Wounds and Trauma

Author and psychic Hollister Rand once told me: "When we make changes in our life here, it affects everyone in the past and everyone in the future." In other words, we not only have the capacity to heal our own wounds, but also those of our ancestors, our children, and generations yet to come. Just as the beating of a butterfly's wings can affect the weather on the other side of the world, so can our spiritual efforts have effects that are much larger and more significant than we can possibly imagine.

Many people speak of a "family curse" like alcoholism, workaholism, teen pregnancy, or adultery. These curses can feel so entrenched that the mere thought of trying to lift them can fill you with despair. After all, if your parents, grandparents, and great-grandparents all went through the same thing, what are the odds that it can really end with you? This despair can feel even more acute when you watch your own children and grandchildren, nieces and nephews, begin to struggle with these very same behaviors.

One client who came to me for help admitted he was a sex addict. He was fifty-four, and had been dealing with the pattern throughout his entire life. Although he had been happily married in his twenties and enjoyed great sex with his wife, he still frequented massage parlors—those he described as having "happy endings." He felt out of control. After he and his first wife divorced, he began dating a number of women and eventually remarried. But that didn't stop him from having affairs during the eight years of this second marriage. He claimed he went through periods of abstinence, but he never felt completely in control. When he came to me, he was about to be married for the third time, was seeing a therapist, and had enrolled in a 12-step program. He seemed very determined to overcome his addiction.

"My dad was the same way," he confessed. "Cheating on my mother all the time. And now my twenty-six-year-old daughter is going down the same road. She's been in a string of short relationships, and doesn't seem to be able to commit to any one person. I feel terrible when I think about this pattern continuing down my family tree—I really wanted it to stop with me."

Watching your descendants enact a pattern that you yourself have struggled to break can be devastating. Yet the ancestral healing work you carry out can have a positive impact on their lives as well, even if you never let them know you are doing it. You can send healing energy back in time to help ancestors who succumbed to this problem, and forward in time to help those who are presently struggling and those still to come. The exercises that follow can help you do exactly that.

Exercise: Finding the Source

This exercise is adapted from one developed by David Furlong in his book *Healing Your Ancestral Patterns.*

Start by laying out the family tree you built in chapter 1 in front of where you are seated. Close your eyes for a few moments and notice the rhythm of your breath and your heartbeat. Let your breathing be natural, but a little deeper and a little slower than usual. Relax and think of a pattern you would like to release—physical, emotional, behavioral, or psychological. As you sit quietly, call on any loving ancestors you want to have with you.

With your eyes closed, imagine two chairs side by side in front of you, with your mother in one and your father in the other. You may see them sitting there in your mind's eye, or sense their presence, or just know that they are with you.

As you consider your mother, be aware of any thoughts or feelings that come up. If you can visualize her, what does she look like? If she has already passed on, is she the age she was when she died? Or does she look younger? When you sense her presence, how do you react? Is there anything she is trying to communicate to you right now? Then move on to your father and go through the same process.

With your eyes still closed, imagine a row of four chairs directly behind your parents in which you see your four grandparents. Even if you didn't know your grandparents, try to see or sense their presence in those chairs. Repeat the same process you followed with your parents. Then imagine a third row of eight chairs behind your grandparents with your great-grandparents seated there. Many of us never knew our great-grandparents, but that doesn't matter. Imagine their presence anyway. See which great-grandparent, if any, you sense most strongly.

Sitting in these three rows of chairs are the fourteen ancestors who are your direct progenitors. As you gaze at them, bring your focus to the pattern for which you seek healing, and ask Spirit to identify the person who most strongly carried the wound you are addressing. Once you've stated your request, this ancestor may stand up, or a beacon of light may highlight them, or everyone else except this ancestor may fade away.

Exercise: Healing a Family Curse

Call to mind the ancestor you identified in the previous exercise. Close your eyes and see and feel a stream of light and love filling your being. Once you feel completely full of light and love, lift both your hands, with your fingers pointing up and your palms out. Sit up straight so that your heart is open, and send the love and light to your ancestor.

Feel this power flowing from the palms of your hands and your heart directly to your ancestor. Don't direct it at the wound; rather, channel it toward the ancestor for them to receive. Continue this process for three to five minutes, or until it feels complete.

If for some reason you feel that your ancestor is unable to receive your healing energy—or that you are unable to send it—review the exercises given in chapter 6 on forgiveness. If you carry any lingering negative feelings toward this person, it will impede the healing process, so it's best to take care of those first, then return to this exercise and try again.

Once you have finished sending love and light to your ancestor, relax your hands in your lap, palms facing up. Observe how your own light and love return this healing energy to you. Allow yourself simply to receive it through your heart, your hands, and your third eye. Feel the power of the light and love envelop you and fill you up in a pleasant and beneficial way.

Finally, release your ancestor with gratitude for participating in this healing. Notice any reaction as they fade away. Be sure to record your experience in your journal.

Exercise: Healing Your Descendants

Now let's go one step further and bring this healing forward to future generations. As in the previous exercise, fill yourself with love and light. Raise your hands into the giving position, with palms facing out and fingers pointing up. Call to mind the wound you healed in the previous exercise and see yourself sending that healing energy forward to your descendants—both those now living and those yet to come. You may also choose to send this energy to your siblings.

As you set this intention, note how the power of the healing light and love is once again channeled through your hands and heart. Please note that, other than setting the intention to send this powerful light and love to your descendants, you don't need to try and heal this wound in those who follow you. The energy you've sent will do what is necessary to heal them. Trust that this energy can move across time and space, backward and forward.

After a few minutes, allow your hands to relax in your lap. Take a few slow, deep breaths, and feel your body release any tension that developed during this process. Let it drift down your body, through your legs and feet, and into the ground.

Over time, you may witness some changes in your descendants as a result of this practice. Don't tell them what you've been doing; just be a patient observer of any changes that may occur. You have provided a blessing, not only for yourself, but also for those who came before you and for those yet to come.

Emotional Catharsis

Healing ancestral wounds can sometimes take the form of emotional catharsis—a powerful experience in which you feel your pain deeply and release it more fully than you've been able to before. Catharsis often happens in the context of therapy, with the support of a trained professional, but you can also achieve it on your own during periods of deep self-reflection, or during or after meaningful conversations with friends or relatives. Even if you have a solid intellectual understanding of your ancestral patterns, it can take courage and preparation to face the deep feelings required for true catharsis.

In a conversation I once had with an acquaintance, the subject of my childhood came up. Although this is not a subject I normally discuss with near-strangers, the woman in question was very intuitive, so I opened up to her, telling her about my experience as the "invisible child" of a mother who had mixed feelings about being a parent at all. It was my unspoken assignment to stay out of trouble and not be seen, and I got very, very good at these tasks. As I shared my memories of being a shy and rather unusual child, I began to feel the intense, familiar sadness that always came up when I reflected on the fact that my mother never really knew me for the person I was.

After this conversation, I felt rattled and emotionally activated. So many old memories and traumas had been stirred up that I felt a little disembodied and ungrounded. When I got home, I was still in a semi-trance state and moving very slowly. I sat down at the table and began to write, letting my hand move freely across the page with no filter or self-consciousness. As I wrote, I started to cry, eventually sinking into a deep, deep sobbing. Small pools of tears formed here and there on the paper. I didn't bother to wipe them away.

Then I heard my mother's voice. She was speaking to me as clearly as if she were only a foot away. I felt her presence strongly and knew it was actually her spirit from the other side. She said: "Ah, Steve! *Now* I see you! Now I understand!" These words touched me so deeply that the grief that had been embedded in my body and my heart for my whole life began gushing out even more intensely. My sobbing became uncontrollable and I heard wailing that, although I knew was my own, seemed distant, as if it were coming from somewhere else.

The blessing my mother provided in that moment healed a deep wound that had become scarred over through time. I realized I'd been playing out an ancestral "mother wound," hiding my true self under a veil of shame. The experience of being fully seen and acknowledged by the woman who birthed me and nurtured me through childhood allowed me to reveal more of my inner workings, my true self. Even though I still experienced some pockets of resistance, I began to feel more relaxed about showing up without any disguises.

The exercise that follows can lead you to your own moment of healing with an ancestor, paving the way to profound emotional catharsis.

Exercise: What Do You Need to Hear?

Think of an ancestor with whom you have unfinished emotional business—for example, a parent who let you down in some way, or whose actions caused you pain. Ask yourself what you most need to hear from this person. For example: "I finally see you," or "I'm proud of you," or "I'm sorry and I love you."

Then close your eyes and call this ancestor into your mind. Imagine this person approaching you at whatever distance feels safe and saying these words to you with total and complete sincerity. Allow yourself to feel the cascade of emotions as these long-awaited words penetrate your heart and mind. You may feel the need to cry or lie down; you may want to dance or shake. Give yourself time to experience whatever energies arise in this moment fully, whether that takes minutes or hours. What does it feel like to finally hear these words from your ancestor? How will this change your life—not only your future, but your past?

Know that your ancestor is now in a higher realm in which he or she can see clearly and gain new perspectives on past mistakes. Even though you carried out this ritual in your imagination, know that its effects are real—and that your ancestor is working *with* your imagination to help bring about this healing.

You can repeat this exercise as often as necessary, with as many ancestors as you like. Always be sure to record your experiences in your journal so you can reflect on them later.

Energy Healing

Physicists tell us that everything on this planet is energy, some of which has manifested as physical form. They refer to this phenomenon as the "unified field"—the plane on which all things are connected, no matter where they occur in time or space. The existence of the unified field means that we, as physical creatures derived from this universal energy, can connect to anything we choose using the power of our consciousness. This is why practices like visualization, shamanic journeying, and energy healing can be so powerful for so many people.

With preparation and intention, your consciousness can reach across the unified field to connect with ancestors, no matter how many years, decades, or even centuries they have been gone from this earth. In fact, the existence of this energetic field means that the energy of your consciousness is *already* intertwined with theirs. Moreover, you and your ancestors are both interwoven into the larger field of consciousness itself, which has an infinite number of force lines going every which way throughout the universe. As author Judith Rich writes:

> As you transform, the energy of the entire lineage preceding you is transformed, for it is all happening now through you, as you. You are the one who can heal old wounds for your entire lineage, forgive old enemies, shift conditioning and beliefs, release pain that has held preceding generations captive for centuries.

Making this powerful connection requires only your focused intention and the relaxed vigilance that comes from a more meditative state of mind.

The benefit of healing any ancestral wound is that you and your descendants will in turn be healed. The healing you send out into the unified field naturally comes back to you, in a virtuous cycle of giving and receiving. The exercise below can help you tap into this cycle.

Exercise: Ancestral Energy Healing

If you have already worked with one or more types of energy healing, you may find this exercise relatively easy. If energy healing is new to you, try it with an ancestor following the steps below. As always, I encourage you to "be your own scientist"—experiment to find what works for you.

Start by taking out the family tree you created in chapter 1 and setting it in front of you. Take three full, deep breaths, then scan your body and simply observe any sensations you find. Pay particular attention to sensing your feet connecting with the ground. Elevate your rib cage so your breath can flow easily and effortlessly, then lift the crown of your head toward the sky and feel the power of the Earth Mother and Sky Father entering your physical body and filling your soul body.

When you are ready, open your eyes and call for any ancestor who needs healing by saying: "I am here to be of service to any healing that is needed for any of my ancestors. Please come forward." Wait patiently for a few moments. Gaze at your family tree and see where your eyes land.

If your primary perceptual mode is clairsentience—if you perceive most easily through your physical senses—slowly pass your hand a couple of inches above your family tree until you sense which ancestor is responding to your offer. This may manifest as a tingling, a warmth, a coolness, or another sensation in the hand that is scanning. If you're more cognitively oriented, you may just *know* which ancestor is heeding your call. If you've copied your family tree onto index cards, shuffle them and draw one, trusting that this is the ancestor to whom you'll be sending healing energy.

Thank the ancestor with whom you'll be working for coming forward. Imagine him or her sitting or standing across from you. Close your eyes and call on a memory of a time when you were filled with love and compassion—the birth of a child, a romantic alliance, or any experience where you felt deep compassion and love for someone. Note how your body feels and especially how your heart responds.

Lift your hands, with your fingers facing up and your palms out, and point them toward your ancestor. Send energy through the palms of your hands and through your heart. Stay with the sensations that you brought to the fore as you recalled an instance when you felt deep love and compassion.

In your mind or out loud, softly repeat the phrase: "Healing, healing, healing." Note what your ancestor does as he or she receives your loving energy. Stay focused on the process without thinking about the results. Just see what you see, hear what you hear, and feel what you feel. Take your time. Maintain this focus for at least five to ten minutes for best results.

Once you feel complete, relax your hands in your lap. Look around the room, as this will help you come out of your meditative state and orient you back to the here and now. Thank your ancestor for receiving this gift of healing energy from you. If possible, go outside and connect with nature to help you get grounded and oriented.

Once you've completed your healing session, write about your experience in your journal. Notice particularly anything you may have learned about the ancestor to whom you sent the healing energy.

Chapter 8

Shamanic Journeying

Ever since I undertook my shamanic training many decades ago, my primary spiritual discipline has been the shamanic journey. Shamanic journeys involve inducing a mildly altered state of consciousness in which you can meet and interact with deep aspects of yourself and your own intuition, as well as with ancestors, spirit guides, power animals, and any other figures that may be important to you. These journeys have been practiced in many cultures around the world in order to gain information, bring about healing, and impart guidance that can't always be accessed with the ordinary thinking mind.

Many of these journeys follow a basic pattern. Shamans open sacred space by making a gesture or series of gestures indicating that they are preparing to leave their ordinary consciousness. Then they set their intention and induce a mild trance state by drumming or rattling. When ready, they follow a visualization sequence that leads them deep into their own subconscious. Once there, they may experience visions, hear words or sounds, feel physical sensations, or access hard-to-describe insights or flashes of knowingness—the four channels for receiving information discussed in chapter 5. They may see themselves carrying out tasks or rituals that have deep symbolic meaning. Once they have completed the journey, they come back to their ordinary state of consciousness and close the sacred space with a ritual gesture or series of gestures that indicates they have returned.

Shamanic journeys are a great way to connect with your ancestors, whether or not you knew them well when they were alive. Indeed, they are a great way to connect with ancestors who walked the earth long before you were born, and with ancestors so ancient they seem to belong to another level of being entirely. It comes as a revelation to many that they can always meet their ancestors in the deep inner space of a shamanic journey, no matter how long ago they departed from the earth. Although this type of journeying may feel strange or unfamiliar to you at first, you may soon find that it becomes one of your favorite practices for working with ancestral patterns.

The messages you receive during a shamanic journey may be direct, like a verbal statement from an ancestor, or they may be symbolic and require some thoughtful deciphering. The wonderful thing about these journeys is that you can do them as many times as you like, returning to visit certain ancestors again and again and developing relationships with them. As you open up communication channels over time, the messages you receive will become easier to interpret. You may be surprised to discover that your ancestors sometimes carry very different energy when encountered in a shamanic journey than they did during their time on earth, because they have gained wisdom and compassion in the afterlife. For many, this is a profoundly healing experience.

Journey to My Father

After my father passed away, I took a shamanic journey to visit his spirit. When he appeared, I found myself tearing up, thinking about how much I missed him. He approached and began to talk to me with great kindness in his voice, giving me this message:

Hold your head up and know you're on the right track. I love what you're doing. You have helped me heal greatly since my death. Your tears right now help us all heal—myself and several others. You grieve for us, but you have no need to. I am happy. If you could just be this happy you would know. I don't feel things in the way you do as a living being. Know that I am not dead. I live in your heart and the hearts of others, whether they're aware of it or not.

As I listened in amazement, he went on:

While I was alive, I loved you. I did. I just didn't show it. Please don't judge anyone in our lineage. There's so much that goes into being human. The soul carries its own destiny, as you know.

Then he told me about his relationship with his own parents and with the earth. He gave me advice about my own relationship with my wife and her children, and urged me to connect with my young grandson, who needed a strong male influence in his life. He concluded by saying:

Steven, you are a jewel. You're doing so much for so many even though you underrate it. I cannot be in your world of ordinary reality, but I am watching you and taking care of all of my kin. Thank you for all you are doing. We all thank you.

After my father finished speaking, he stepped aside. Behind him, I saw dozens of ancestors, not all of whom I recognized. My mother came forward. She didn't say anything—just smiled. I saw her mouth the words "I love you"—words I never heard her say in real life. Finally, my grandfather stepped into the light. Of all the grandchildren, I was his favorite. He smiled at me as well, and I saw a white glow around him—perhaps a sign that he was completing his spiritual evolution in the afterlife.

I came away from this experience feeling even more appreciative of my ancestors, especially my father. I had received his blessing and heard the kind words that he had never spoken to me while he was in the world of the living. He had obviously come a long way in the afterlife, and I found it reassuring to know that he was watching over our family. As for my grandson, I heeded his great-grandfather's words and began to make regular contact.

Soon, that relationship became a very important part of my life, and I was so grateful that I had followed my father's advice.

Hollister Rand, author of *I'm Not Dead, I'm Different,* once told me: "We think we build bridges to our ancestors, but the truth is, they build bridges to us and try to reach us." I would add that connecting with your ancestors in a shamanic journey only requires you to be open to possibilities, and stay tuned in to their messages in whatever form they come.

Shamanic journeys can help you access insights and intuitions that aren't always available to your thinking mind. You can have profound encounters with ancestors in this ceremonial space, even if you never met them in "real" life. In the following exercise, I give you the basic framework for a shamanic journey. Once you are familiar with it, try journeying to meet an ancestor. Then come up with variations that resonate with your own spiritual and aesthetic preferences.

Exercise: Journeying to Meet an Ancestor

For this exercise, all you need is a quiet, private space and a drum or rattle. If you do not have a drum or rattle, you can play a recorded shamanic drumming track. There are many of these available online.

Start by establishing sacred space. In other words, make a ritual gesture that feels meaningful to you, indicating that you are setting aside your ordinary mind and everyday concerns, and undertaking an inner journey. For some, this means sweeping the floor and lighting candles; for others, it means laying down a circle of flower petals. The possibilities are endless. If you are journeying to meet a specific ancestor, you may want to set up a photograph of that person as part of your space-setting ritual.

Once your sacred space is ready, state your intention for the journey. For example: "I wish to journey to a place where I can meet the spirit of my great-grandmother." You can ask for advice on a specific issue—something like: "I wish to meet an ancestor who can give me insight into my ancestral pattern of failing to commit in intimate relationships." Or your intention can be more broad and general. The important thing is to keep it simple. Don't complicate it by asking too many different questions all at once. Remember, you can always take another journey with a different intention.

When you are ready, begin to play your drum or rattle, or start your recording. Close your eyes and let the rhythm wash over you. For a few moments, simply listen to the sound. Let the rhythm slip you gently into an altered state. Imagine that a trusted guide is escorting you to meet your ancestor. This guide may take the form of a human being, an animal, a mythical creature like a dragon, or it may appear simply as a color or as light. As your journey proceeds, this protective being will stay at your side, looking out for you.

Visualize your guide leading you through a portal—a door, a tunnel, or a hollow log. On the other side of this portal, you find the spirit of your ancestor. If this spirit doesn't arrive right away, just wait and be patient. When your ancestor appears, they may look and sound the same as they did in life, or they may take an entirely different form. They may speak in words, or communicate through gestures, sounds, images, or even scents. Be open to whatever arises. Stay with your ancestor as long as feels right. When you feel ready to go, express your thanks and let your guide lead you back through the portal and into the ordinary world.

Slowly let your drumming or rattling fade and stop. Open your eyes and feel yourself returning to your body in the present. Wiggle your toes; feel the sensation of your feet on the ground. Know that you are back in the familiar realm of your everyday life. Then close your sacred space by blowing out candles, folding up your blanket, or making any other gesture that feels meaningful to you and that represents that you have fully returned to an ordinary state of consciousness.

Write down any messages you received in your journal, and know that you can always journey again to seek further clarity or to visit other ancestors.

Exercise: Calling the Ancestors

While on shamanic journeys, some people like to call their ancestors by chanting or singing. The following is a simple song that will invite the ancestors to come to you. Sing the first two lines in a monotone, then chant the last line in three descending tones. You can sing this song after you open your sacred space, before you begin to drum.

> *Ancestors, ancestors, we are calling.*
> *Ancestors, ancestors, we are calling.*
> *Come! Come! Come!*

Repeat this song at least four times. You'll find that the rhythm and sound begin to take on a life of their own.

Ancestor Sitting and Ancestor Walking

In his book *Shamanism as a Spiritual Practice for Daily Life*, shamanic practitioner Tom Cowan described how he received an inspiration one day while walking through the woods—an experiential awareness of what it must have been like to actually *be* an ancestor. He realized that, just as he was walking under the trees, his ancestors had also walked in the forest. Just as he was breathing in the forest air, with its aroma of decomposing leaves and fungi, his ancestors had inhaled this wonderful, life-giving scent. And he extended that insight to the modern world as well. When he heard a plane fly overhead, he intuitively understood that, even as he could hear others traveling around him, his ancestors had heard others traveling around them as well.

Cowan was inspired to develop these insights into a shamanic practice that placed the ordinary events of his life in a larger social and historical context. Whereas we in the West are brought up to see ourselves as individuals, this practice reminds us that we are part of a long chain of humanity—that we all share what I call "ancestral consciousness." In fact, every generation is merely a variation on an essential theme. Even though the environmental and technological conditions of our ancestors may have been very different from our own, we nevertheless have many experiences in common with them.

I have a small area outside my home where I do my writing. Directly across from me on the other side of the yard is an exquisite melaleuca tree, sometimes called a tea tree. She stretches sideways from her spot in the corner of the lot, her skin exposed in places where her bark is peeling away. One day, I decided to try reaching out to my ancestral consciousness sitting beneath this tree and seeing where she led me.

I slowed my breath, gazed up at her branches, and began to feel her solid presence. I said to myself: "I am appreciating the solidness of this tree as my ancestors appreciated the solidness of trees." Then I noticed her ability to yield to the wind: "I notice this tree's ability to sway in the wind, just as my ancestors noticed that trees sway in the wind." I felt as if I were breathing with the tree: "I am breathing with this tree just as my ancestors breathed with trees." I noticed the sound of a barn owl somewhere close by: "I am hearing an owl as my ancestors heard the call of owls."

After a short while, I got up and walked around the yard and continued viewing and sensing from this state of ancestral consciousness. Even in my relatively small backyard, I experienced timeless moments in which it felt as if I actually *were* an ancestor experiencing this environment! This went on for a few minutes, then I went inside.

And as I went, I made the statement: "I am going into shelter just as my ancestors went into shelters."

The meditation below will take you beyond words and intellect into a physical and sensory empathic experience of what life was like for your long-ago ancestors. It gives you an opportunity to engage all your senses to experience intimately what your ancestors did, and to access the ancestral consciousness that is deeply embedded in your DNA.

Exercise: Ancestor Sitting Meditation

Find a comfortable spot outdoors—in your backyard, a nearby park, or a wooded area. You can sit in a chair or on the ground, but make sure you sit with your rib cage lifted so your heart is open and your breathing is easy.

Notice your heartbeat. Observe the rise and the fall of your chest and stomach as you breathe easily and effortlessly. Close your eyes and repeat this phrase slowly ten times: "I am breathing just as my ancestors breathed."

When you are ready, open your eyes and look around. Notice the natural elements of your environment—soil, trees, water, stones, mountains. With each observation, make a statement like: "I am seeing this soil just as my ancestors saw this soil." "I am seeing these clouds as my ancestors saw the clouds." "I am seeing this tree as my ancestors saw a tree." "I am feeling my feet on the ground just as my ancestors felt their feet on the ground."

Continue making these kinds of statements about any natural elements that enter your field of awareness. If you find you're repeating statements, that's quite all right. Continue doing so until something fresh comes to mind. When you feel complete, simply stop and breathe quietly, allowing your new awareness to settle.

You can also do this meditation walking in an outdoor area like a park, or in the mountains or a wooded area, or even in your backyard. If possible, take off your shoes and go barefoot, or else wear leather-soled shoes, as these will connect you with the earth, whereas rubber-soled shoes will insulate you from that connection.

Start to walk more slowly than your usual pace. As you walk, make note of anything in your environment or sensory experience, and connect it to your ancestors. If you stop to pick berries or mushrooms, or sit on a log to rest, or pause at a spring to drink, reflect on the fact that these are all acts your ancestors did before you. If you encounter animals or people, simply note the fact that your ancestors had these encounters as well.

Use your imagination to feel that you are truly an ancestor experiencing these things as you walk slowly through the environment.

Chapter 9

Stepping Back

In his book *The Spiral of Memory and Belonging*, shamanic teacher Frank MacEowen writes of a dream he had in which he hugged his father, only to find himself "stepping back" into his father's body and seeing through his father's eyes. Next, he stepped back into his grandfather's body, and then his great-grandfather's, until he finally arrived at a very ancient being he described as a "primal ancestor." MacEowen writes:

> Suddenly I felt a healing energy, almost as if this primal ancestor were sending a prayer through the family line of men, attempting to clear up some things that needed resolution.

The experience of literally seeing through his ancestors' eyes helped MacEowen understand his ancestral patterns, and led him to do extensive shamanic and inner work to heal them.

Taking the time to imagine what life was like for your ancestors—including stepping back into their bodies and appreciating how it felt to see through their eyes—can open the door to new levels of understanding and compassion. Many times, we don't even consider what it was like to walk the earth as the people who came before us did—the smells and sounds, the physical aches and pains, the hunger and thirst. By stepping back into our ancestor's bodies using shamanic techniques, we can gain valuable information about the aspects of their lives that continue to affect us today. The exercise that follows, which is adapted from MacEowen's book, can help you do just that.

This exercise leads you to a greater awareness of what your ancestors experienced with their physical senses, and strengthens your relationship with them. It also provides an opportunity to get acquainted with one of the the Elders—what MacEowen calls "primal ancestors." These Elders reside so far back in our family trees that they are truly related to us all, and sharing the wisdom and perspective they embody can be a life-changing experience.

Exercise: Stepping Back to an Elder

I have simplified this exercise to make it more accessible to solitary practitioners, although it can be performed in large groups led by a facilitator.

All you need for this exercise is a room large enough so you can walk at least five steps with no obstructions, some recorded instrumental music, something to cover your eyes, and loose, comfortable clothing.

The exercise consists of five stages. You start by reaching out to one of your parents, then "step back" in stages to one of the Old Ones, an Elder. It doesn't matter which side of your family you choose to work with. In fact, you can leave that an open question until you start the process and allow your intuition to determine whether you start with your mother or your father. Don't worry about whether you personally know any of these ancestors. It's unlikely you knew your great-great-grandparents when they were alive. But you now have the opportunity to get to know them as ancestors.

Start your music and, standing straight and tall, either close your eyes or cover them in some way. Notice your breathing, your heartbeat, and any other sensations in your body. Notice any areas of tension.

When you are ready, take a step backward about a foot. Imagine that you are now standing in the body of one of your parents. Which parent did you intuitively choose? Let's assume you chose your father. What is it like to stand in his body? Do you feel safe and comfortable?

To the best of your ability, allow your body to express your father's posture. How does that make you feel? For a moment, notice any images, sensations, or thoughts that come to you as you inhabit his physical space. How does your father feel toward you? How did he show love? What were his hopes and dreams? What made him happy? What were his struggles? What wounds did he carry? What resources were available to help deal with his struggles and wounds? What characteristics and qualities were passed on to you? What talents or abilities can he offer you today? What was his relationship with the land? What was his relationship with his own parents?

Continue breathing easily and steadily, and take a little time to allow any images, feelings, sensations, or thoughts to come to you. Did you gain any new insights or revelations about your father that had never occurred to you before? Know that you can always return to this space to seek more information.

When you're ready, take another step back and imagine you are standing in the body of one of your grandparents. What is it like standing in the body of this ancestor? Do you feel safe and comfortable? To the best of your ability, allow your body to express this grandparent's posture. How does that make you feel? Notice any images, sensations, or thoughts that come to you as you share this physical space, and ask yourself the same questions as above. Know that you can access this experience any time you want to know your grandparent in a new way.

Repeat this process three more times, entering a great-grandparent, a great-great-grandparent, and finally, an Elder. This Elder lived a life very different from yours, in a world very different from yours—close to the land, the seasons, and the natural rhythms of the Earth Mother. Technologies like computers and automobiles were unknown; instead, this being was surrounded by trees, stones, and wild-flowing water.

Assume the posture of this Elder and be aware of what this feels like. Let your hands form a gesture that expresses their energy and presence, and make note of it. What information are you receiving? What does this spirit want you to know?

Consider making a commitment to the Elder to renew your contact on a regular basis, to remain aware of this spirit as much of the time as possible, and to get to know more about it. If you agree to this, let this ancient ancestor know in some way. Is there some quality that this Elder can help you develop in yourself?

Take a few more moments to allow any images, feelings, sensations, or thoughts to come to you as you breathe easily and steadily. Know that you can meet with this Elder anytime. Be sure to record your experience in your journal.

Embodying Ancestors

Although many ancestral healing practices involve visualization or written or verbal dialogue, profound healing can also occur through the body, with no thinking or speaking required. When we invite our ancestors into our bodies—when we embody them—we can share with them whatever healing we ourselves are experiencing on a somatic level.

I have a client who is a certified aquatic massage therapist. She practices a technique commonly known as Watsu, which combines movement, stretches, and massage in a pool of water warmed to near-body temperature. She moves her patients around slowly and caringly in the water, allowing their bodies to find their own natural rhythm in a state of deep relaxation. During these sessions, many people find themselves entering an altered state.

One day when she herself was receiving a Watsu session from another therapist, she suddenly entered into a sacred experience with her ancestors. As the therapist cradled her like an infant and rocked her slowly back and forth in the water, she suddenly felt herself *becoming* her grandmother. It felt as if her grandmother were receiving the healing experience. Then the experience shifted to focus on her aunt, and finally her mother.

When she felt herself becoming her mother, she began to sob. She connected with her mother's ways of shutting down, and experienced her eventually being able to receive nurturing touch and healing. She felt as if her own body had become a channel through which her mother could be healed. She realized that she had nurtured her own daughter more than her mother had ever nurtured her. Then she sensed that she had received more nurturing from her mother than her mother had received from her own mother—her grandmother. The embodiment that was taking place was, in fact, delivering healing to ancestors at least four generations back, probably more. Then she felt herself shifting back into her own body at a time when she was very young, and she felt incredibly loved and loving. As the Watsu session ended, she melted into a deep sense of gratitude that she had been able to give this gift to her mother and grandmother—and to herself.

This client's story demonstrates how profound instances of ancestral healing can occur when you least expect them. She knew that her mother and aunt had unhealed wounds, and that it was likely that her grandmother and great-grandmother did as well. The experience of being cradled and rocked so lovingly in the warm water provided an opportunity for all of these ancestors to come in and receive from and through her the nurturing they needed to move ahead on their own journey of healing in the afterlife.

In the following exercise, you'll find some ideas for how to bring these powerful moments into your own life.

Exercise: Embodied Ancestor Healing

Think of an ancestor whose trauma manifested as physical stiffness, rigidity, or difficulty giving or receiving affection, then plan an experience you find physically pleasurable—getting a massage, going for a swim, or dancing to your favorite music, for example. As you partake in this experience, imagine that your ancestor is also receiving the pleasure and joy you feel in your own body. You can even say to yourself: "Just as I am enjoying the warm sunlight on my skin, may my ancestor also enjoy it," or "Just as I am moving my body to the music, may my ancestor also feel the happiness of dancing."

Allow yourself to feel that it is not you, but your ancestor who is receiving the massage, or going for the swim, or enjoying the dance. If you like, you can work with several ancestors in turn, giving each one a chance to enjoy the pleasurable experience. When you are ready to end the exercise, be sure to return to your own body. Feel the sense of calm and gratitude that arises, knowing that your ancestors have shared in your healing. Record your impressions in your journal.

Chapter 10

Connecting with Ancestral Spirits

In chapter 5, we talked about channels through which we receive messages from ancestors in the spirit world, In this chapter, we'll look at several specific techniques that can help you open up channels of communication with your ancestors and understand the spirit messages they are sending you.

Divination

Divination is a method for accessing intuitive information through external sources. The root of the word—*divine*—literally means "from God," although some people believe that the messages they receive through divination come from spirits who have crossed over or from their own higher self. Divination has been around for as long as human beings have inhabited the planet, and just about everything has been used in its practice—tea leaves, clouds, animal behavior, pendulums, and items like stones, cards, and sticks. These practices often require skilled interpretation or the use of manuals or handbooks.

You may already be familiar with the divination tools discussed below, and any of them can be used for connecting with ancestors. You can consult them to discover the information, insights, and guidance you need to heal your ancestral patterns.

Tarot cards have been around for thousands of years, at least since ancient Egypt. They were first used in the West during the Middle Ages. Most tarot decks consist of seventy-eight cards divided into four suits. When laid out in spreads, these cards deliver messages that a trained reader can interpret. Oracle cards, on the other hand, are more straightforward and many find them simpler to use. Oracle cards are very user-friendly, and even novices find that, with some practice, they can become quite adept at performing readings for themselves and others. Both tarot and oracle decks are typically accompanied by guidebooks that provide directions for how to use and interpret the cards.

Runes are symbols drawn from pre-Latin alphabets that date back to the second century. Each of these ancient symbols is typically drawn on small ceramic stones or embedded in small, smooth pieces of glass. Each rune represents not only a word, but also deeper layers of meaning associated with keywords that can be discerned intuitively. These days, runes most often come with a booklet that gives guidelines for interpreting the keywords they represent.

The *I Ching* is one of the oldest divination tools still available. It is based on a fairly complex system of sixty-four hexagrams that is over four thousand years old. Readings entail throwing bundles of yarrow stalks to produce apparently random sets of numbers, each of which corresponds to a hexagram whose meaning can be found in the *I Ching*. There are any number of books that describe how to use the *I Ching*. One of my personal favorites is *The I Ching Workbook* by R. L. Wing.

Divining with any of these tools to receive and understand messages from ancestors involves an intuitive collaboration between you, the ancestor, and the tool itself. Many people find that the hardest part of using these practices is learning to trust their own intuition. Although there are many guidebooks that can help with interpreting messages, the key to understanding the messages these techniques provide is to consider what is relevant to you. In other words, does the guidance you receive make sense at an intuitive level? Does it resonate with you?

You may find that some messages you receive through divination strike a chord and some don't. These tools aren't typically designed to give you straightforward "yes" or "no" answers. But when used properly, they can be accurate enough to give you some guidance and direction, or at least some ideas as to how you can discover the answers you seek. My rule of thumb is that if roughly 80 percent of my readings make sense, then I'm likely to use that method again. I recommend doing readings for yourself every few days to see what your experience is like.

Divining with My Father

I recently used a set of runes to have a conversation with my father, who died several decades ago. I decided to keep the session open-ended, simply asking him for guidance and requesting that he tell me anything he wanted me to know. I began the session by saying aloud: "My beloved ancestor, my father, I'd like a message that is clear, concise, helpful, and healing."

After I made my request, I drew a rune named Inguz, whose keywords are "fertility" and "new beginnings." According R. H. Blum in his *Book of Runes*, drawing this rune may "mark a time of joyful deliverance, of new life, a new path." Blum goes on to say that Inguz often shows up when it's time to complete a project.

Meditating on this rune, I realized that my father was telling me that publishing this book must be my top priority. I had been working on the project in fits and starts, setting it aside for days or weeks at a time. Now, he was telling me to buckle myself in and drive it over the finish line. Reflecting further, I realized that my family had an ancestral pattern of unfinished projects. My family tree was littered with relatives who "couldn't get anything done," even though they had great ideas and boatloads of talent. Indeed, "can't get anything done" was one of our dark laws. By showing me this rune, my father was encouraging me to break this pattern, not only for myself, but for our entire lineage.

After this divination session, I made a conscious commitment to work on my book for at least two hours a day until it was finished. A month or two later, I had completed the manuscript and sent it to my publisher. My father's message helped me shift an ancestral pattern and dissolve one of my dark laws. All I had to do was listen and put his advice into practice.

Below is an exercise that can help you receive spirit messages through divination to find the guidance you need.

Exercise: Divining with an Ancestor

Choose any divination tool that feels meaningful to you, and identify an ancestor with whom you'd like to communicate. If you don't have a specific ancestor in mind, you can request messages from any ancestor who comes forward.

Begin by sitting quietly for a few moments with your eyes closed and the divination tool before you, then focus on a question you want to ask your ancestor. If you don't have a specific question in mind, ask for a general message by saying out loud: "Beloved ancestor, _____ (ancestor's name), I'd like a message that is clear, concise, helpful, and healing." If the question is for any ancestor who comes forward, you can say: "Beloved ancestors, I'd like a message that is clear, concise, helpful, and healing."

Use your divination tool according to its instructions, whether that means laying out cards, tossing sticks, or some other method. Once you've set out the piece or pieces, take a few moments simply to contemplate them. What impressions do you get? How do you feel when you look at them? Do any impressions come to mind, even before consulting a guidebook for an interpretation? What about physical sensations in your body?

Then consult a trusted manual to interpret your results. Are you surprised at the response? Does any of it resonate with you? What do you think your ancestors are trying to tell you? Take a few minutes to jot down your impressions in your journal.

If you are new to divination, attempt this type of communication with an ancestor every few days. The more you practice, the easier it becomes. I encourage you to experiment with several different divination practices, knowing that you may eventually settle on a particular tool that works best for you.

Automatic Writing

One of the oldest forms of connecting with Spirit is through automatic writing, the practice of writing down words and sentences that do not come from your own conscious thoughts. This practice was developed around 420 CE in China, and has been used ever since in various cultures around the world. In the United States, automatic writing experienced a resurgence of popularity in the 1920s when luminaries like Arthur Conan Doyle endorsed the practice.

When you use automatic writing, although it is your hand holding the pen and moving across the page, you are merely transcribing messages from Spirit, not coming up with those messages yourself. This can be a profound way of communicating with an ancestor. You may be amazed to find yourself transcribing messages that come from your great-grandparents or beyond, and you may return to this practice whenever you yearn for a sense of guidance or connection.

If you've never tried automatic writing, it may feel a little strange at first. But don't be discouraged if it doesn't work right away. With just a little practice, you will become more comfortable with the technique. When I've done this, it feels as if my hand is moving of its own free will. Sometimes the writing ends up being somewhat scribbly, but it is always decipherable. The two exercises below can help you become proficient at connecting with the spirit world using this practice.

Exercise: Channeling Spirit Messages

Find a quiet place where you won't be disturbed, with a table or desk upon which you can write. Light a candle and, if you wish, place a couple photos of your ancestors on the table. I strongly suggest you use a pen and paper for this exercise, as you will feel the writing more directly than you would using a computer or similar device.

Once you've established your writing space, sit quietly for a few moments and relax. Allow your breathing to become regular and steady. Close your eyes and say a prayer of thanks to your ancestors. Ask for their blessing for this ceremony.

Now you have some choices to make. You can ask your ancestors a specific question or you can simply ask them for a message. Either way, write down your request at the top of the paper. You can address the question to a particular ancestor, like your mother or grandfather, or you can address your ancestors in general. If this is new to you, you may want to address your mother or father to start.

Once you've written your question and the ancestor's name, lay your pen on the paper and sit quietly. Close your eyes to eliminate any visual distractions. State your request out loud or think it in your mind, directing it to the ancestor you are addressing. Then simply sit still and wait. It may take a few moments before you receive a response. When you feel moved, pick up the pen and start writing. I recommend using your nondominant hand. This may feel rather clumsy, but writing with your nondominant hand helps you to bypass your conscious mind and opens your subconscious mind to act as a channel for the communication.

Allow your hand to travel across the page in whatever way it wants to, without trying to control it. In other words, detach from the process—don't try to make something happen. Just allow whatever happens to happen. Don't try to make sense of the words as you write. You may also find yourself recording symbols or other images. It's important to take your time and not rush this; just allow the ancestor to move your hand as he or she chooses.

Keep your mind as clear as possible by paying attention to your breathing. Keep your breath smooth and natural. If thoughts come up, just notice them and let them pass by. You have become the conduit for communication from your ancestor; stay open and create space for their messages to come through.

Once you're done writing the message, set the paper aside. Stand up and go outside for a short time if possible. Take a walk around your backyard or around the block. When you return, look at what you wrote. Are the messages clear? Do they resonate in some way? Can you decipher the words and symbols in a way that is meaningful to you?

Don't worry if the messages you received don't make sense right away. Set the paper aside and review it in a day or two, or in a week, or in a month. You'll be surprised to discover how the messages come together over time.

Exercise: Creating an Ancestor Dialogue

Once you become comfortable with automatic writing, try creating a dialogue with an ancestor. This requires that you shift back and forth between your usual self and the communications you are receiving from the ancestor.

As in the previous exercise, start by writing out a question and the ancestor's name, then place your pen on the paper and follow the instructions above, allowing your ancestor's response to come through you. When you feel that the message is complete, put down the pen, take a deep breath, and return to your ordinary self.

Once you have fully returned to your ordinary self, write a second question in response to the answer you received. Then shift back into your ancestor's consciousness, allowing his or her message to flow through you. Continue alternating between yourself and your ancestor as many times as needed to complete your dialogue.

Reincarnation and Past Lives

Some traditions teach that the soul reincarnates after a person's death. Many Asian cultures believe that this happens fairly quickly. For instance, when the Dalai Lama dies, it's believed that his soul has already found its way back and the search begins for the boy who is to be the next Dalai Lama.

Occasionally, an ancestor may choose to be reborn into the same family. When this happens, you can have the fascinating experience of becoming your own ancestor. Although it stretches the imagination in an elegant paradox, it's even entirely possible that one or more of your distant ancestors is—well, *you!*

A friend of mine trained with a traditional *sangoma,* or "soul doctor," in Swaziland who shared a story about one of his sons, who was very weak when he was born. Nothing the doctors did seemed to help. He and his wife were very concerned and went to see a trusted sangoma to give them insight into the problem. The soul doctor informed them that their son was, in fact, a reincarnated ancestor who was unhappy with the name they had chosen for him. He insisted that he be named Nduna, which means "elder"—one who is respected, honored, and cherished. In a ritual, the baby was renamed to honor the ancestor and, once the naming ritual was complete, the child became healthy and strong.

This same woman once experienced two different ancestors connecting with her during a drumming and dancing session—ancestors who both claimed to be reincarnations of her. One—an Irish woman with whom she had been working through shamanic journeys for several years—told her she had been a druidic priestess and had reincarnated as my friend in this lifetime. The other was an African ancestor who had first come to her in a past-life soul retrieval. Overcoming her initial confusion about these two spirits and their relationship to her, she eventually began to connect with them both as ancestors and as projections of her own past lives.

Through research, contemplation, and shamanic journeys, I've come to the conclusion that the vast majority of past-life and ancestral memories are one and the same. Memory resides not just in our minds, but also in the very cells of our bodies—and, consequently, in our DNA. Although the farther back we go through the generations, the more diffuse the gene pool is, biologically and spiritually we are still connected to our ancient progenitors, even if only in some small way. We retain some shards of ancestral memory that continue to dwell in us, and we can connect with them through hypnotic regression, shamanic journeys, dreams, and other means. The next two exercises show you ways to make these connections.

Exercise: Past Life Regression

Past life regression is a process whereby those in an altered state of consciousness, typically achieved through hypnosis or a similar meditative practice, connect with a memory of another lifetime that has been embedded deep in their subconscious. By regressing through the past with an intention of finding the source of a particular problem, they can discover the connection between that past life and their present symptoms. This often leads to healing. Past life regressions are best done with the help of an experienced guide, but this exercise can give you a taste of what they are like.

Find a shamanic drumming track online or ask a friend who owns a frame drum to play for you. Once the drumming begins, lie down in a quiet, comfortable place, close your eyes, and take deep, calming breaths.

As you listen to the drumming, imagine that you are floating backward in time. Subtract ten years from your current age and allow yourself to return to that time. Try to really *feel* the same way you felt at that age—in body, mind, and emotions. Then subtract another ten years and put yourself fully into the experience of being yourself at that age. Continue this process until you experience yourself as a newborn baby.

Continue to float back in time, and allow yourself to enter the dark space of the womb, then regress even farther back through the darkness until you feel something tugging you back to earth. When this happens, slowly enter this past life. What sensations do you feel in your body? Do you see images or hear sounds? How old are you? Where are you located on earth? Which historical period does it seem to be? What is happening around you? Are you experiencing a specific event or carrying out a specific task? Don't worry if you don't get all the answers all at once. Remember that you can always come back to this place for more information. For now, a hunch is good enough.

When you feel ready, begin moving forward in time, returning to yourself as a baby, then a child, then a teenager, then an adult, until you arrive back in your present-day body. Write down any impressions you had in your journal. For the next few days and weeks, stay open to signs that give you further clues as to the meaning of what you experienced.

Exercise: Journeying to a Past Life

If you found the exercise above challenging, you may prefer embarking on this simple shamanic journey to meet a past incarnation of yourself. As in the previous exercise, don't worry if you don't get all the answers on your first try. Remember that you can take as many journeys as necessary to explore your past lives fully.

Choose a quiet space where you won't be disturbed. Set your sacred space in your usual way—light incense, shake a rattle, invoke protection from your ancestors, or do anything else that feels meaningful to you. Then sit or lie comfortably and set an intention to meet a previous incarnation of yourself.

If you own a frame drum, begin to drum slowly. If you don't, play a recorded drumming track. Close your eyes and imagine that you and a trusted guide are walking down a long, light-filled tunnel. When you reach the end of the tunnel, you emerge into the Land of the Ancestors. You may find that it is cool and misty, or cold and snowy, or hot and sunny. You may find all kinds of plants and vegetation there. Simply stay open and pay attention to whatever comes up.

Imagine that your guide is leading you to a small bench or log, where you both sit down. Know that if you wait here patiently, your past self will make itself known to you. It may appear in visual form, walking right up to you and introducing itself. Or it may arrive as sound, or as sensation, or as a simple knowing. Allow your past self to connect with you and share as much or as little information about itself as it chooses.

When you feel complete, thank your previous incarnation for showing up. Follow your guide back to the tunnel and make your way through it back to ordinary reality. Let your drumming fade slowly, then come to a stop, or press stop on your recording. End your journey and close your sacred space in a way that feels meaningful to you. Be sure to record what you learned in your journal.

Chapter 11

Crossing Over

Many in the West believe that we stop growing and changing after we die—that the personality we had in life is the one we will continue to express after death. If your uncle was a stern and emotionally reserved person in life, you may expect him to show up as a stern and reserved ancestor in death. Yet sometimes the experience of death changes us. Sometimes we come to embody qualities as ancestors that were less available to us during our earthly lives. Ancestors who were stern and reserved in life may show up as cheerful and relaxed after crossing over, free at last from the heavy burdens that weighed them down in this world. Ancestors who were cold and judgmental in life may finally express compassion, having worked through the inner blockages that prevented them from doing so before.

Sometimes we carry grudges against our ancestors that are rooted in the negative qualities they expressed while they were on earth. When they cross over, we tend to rub their noses in their mistakes rather than supporting them in their ongoing growth toward their higher selves. We forget that they aren't finished with their healing journey, any more than we are finished with ours.

Ancestral Evolution

My friend once received an unexpected visit from the spirit of her father's mother. She had died years before, and the truth was that nobody had gotten along with her very well while she was alive. She had been a tough lady with unyielding opinions on respect and sacrifice, and her choices in life reflected her rigid beliefs. She'd married and had one child—a son—and when that marriage didn't work out, she never remarried. Never even dated. She never stopped loving her ex-husband, and she focused her whole life on raising her son and working hard at odd jobs to make ends meet.

My friend always thought that her grandmother was an unhappy, lonely, and somewhat grumpy woman. She protested whenever her dad insisted that they visit her. So she was somewhat surprised when her grandmother's spirit came to visit her shortly after her own separation and divorce in 2007. At the time, my friend was heartbroken. She felt like she had failed at marriage, and felt awful that her children would have to shuttle back and forth between two homes. Her dream of a true partnership had shattered, leaving her lost and confused.

During that time, she spent an inordinate amount of time meditating, doing intuitive and tarot readings, and attending healing and therapy sessions. She did everything she could to process her experience from a healthy spiritual perspective and avoid sinking into self-pity, blame, or anger. Although she reached out to many friends and relatives for comfort and advice, never in a million years would she have considered calling on her grandmother.

Yet one day, in the midst of a meditation session, her grandmother's spirit came to visit her unexpectedly. My friend recognized her because with her arrival came the aroma of percolated coffee, something she associated only with visiting her grandmother's house. Once she realized who it was, the aroma disappeared, as if her grandmother was satisfied she'd made contact.

My friend's grandmother began to talk to her about their family patterns. She told her that after being so hurt by her first marriage, she vowed she would never love again. From then on, she expressed her love only through criticism, sarcasm, and scolding—things that kept her from getting too close to anyone. My friend felt a sense of relief as her grandmother admitted these behaviors, since those were exactly the reasons she'd never wanted to visit her in life.

Then my friend's grandmother let her know that she was there as an ally to walk her through this difficult time and help her break the family pattern of not letting in love. She implored my friend not to make the same mistake she had. Now that her grandmother had crossed over, she realized that the choice to build walls against love had not served her, but instead had kept her from having what could have been a more joyful and connected life.

My friend's grandmother also pointed out that my friend had withheld love in her marriage as well. Indeed, one of her regular comments to her ex-husband was: "Okay, let's not get too mushy." It wasn't pleasant for my friend to see herself reflected in this way, but it was necessary for her healing. It helped her to realize that she wasn't powerless; she could make changes in the way she related to the people around her in order to construct a different future.

This was a profound experience for my friend. Afterward, she continued to speak to her grandmother periodically. As a result, her memories of a bitter, critical hard-ass were replaced by fond memories of her grandmother's strength and her intense love, which she refused to share out of fear. She even recalled a sweet memory of her grandmother peeling and slicing apples for her because she didn't like the skin—a way of showing love that she had completely forgotten.

My friend's story is a great example of the ways in which our ancestors can evolve after crossing over, both giving healing to their descendants on earth and receiving it in return. Observing my friend's life helped her grandmother realize her own patterns—and ignited an inner determination to keep her granddaughter from making the same mistakes. And listening to her grandmother helped my friend change those patterns in her own life—and for generations to come.

The next exercise can help you do the same for ancestors whose positive qualities may have been hidden or underdeveloped when they were on earth.

Exercise: Imagining Change and Growth

Think of an ancestor about whom you have rather negative memories—a cranky great-aunt, a stingy grandfather. Imagine that this ancestor has recently gone through a tremendous healing experience, receiving whatever was needed in order to release previous pain and come to a profound realization about harmful patterns that shaped his or her life. Let your imagination run wild, picturing this person completely transformed in the best possible ways.

What does this ancestor look like now that they are healed? What does this person's voice sound like? What do they want to tell you?

Imagine this ancestor sharing their realizations with you and seeking your support in healing this family pattern. What does it feel like to allow this person to grow, to change, and to heal? What would it feel like if your own descendants allowed *you* to grow, and change, and heal, regardless of the limitations you've had in this life?

Honoring Ancestors' Graves

In many cultures around the world, honoring the graves of ancestors is an important responsibility and a spiritual practice in its own right. For example, in China, many still celebrate a 2,500-year-old festival called Tomb-Sweeping Day. This early springtime observance gives families the opportunity to honor their ancestors by maintaining their gravesites and making traditional offerings like food and incense. Catholics who visit graves and pray during the first week of November are granted plenary indulgences, while in Egypt, special days are set aside throughout the year for visiting ancestral graves and leaving offerings of rose petals, palm leaves, or fruit.

Honoring your ancestors' graves has benefits for both you and for them. Carefully tended graves let your ancestors know they haven't been forgotten after crossing over, and the conversations you have with them as you tend their graves can deepen your connection and provide opportunities for mutual healing. Tending a gravesite can also remind you of your own mortality, and inspire you to contemplate the things you would like to achieve during your brief stay on earth before you cross over as well.

I have experienced some of my most profound interactions with my ancestors during visits to their graves. For me, this is a quiet and intimate time when I set aside the distractions of my day-to-day life to be with them in their resting place. I've found that the relationships I had with my relatives when they were alive don't end when they cross over, but rather transform. I can still go to them for guidance and advice, or just for a sense of a loving presence.

If you live far from your ancestors' graves, or you come from a tradition in which remains are cremated, you can still honor them by creating an ancestral altar in your home. Although some spiritual traditions do place importance on being in close proximity to the literal bones of their ancestors, you can achieve many of the same benefits by simply showing reverence in a place of your choosing, while keeping the memory of your ancestors alive.

In many cultures, it is common to honor those who have crossed over by creating an ancestral altar in the home—a small table or other dedicated space where photographs of ancestors are displayed and offerings are made on a regular basis. Just as when you tend a grave, creating and tending an altar can signal to your ancestors that you have not forgotten them.

Moreover, an altar can serve as a daily reminder to you that you do not walk through life alone, even if your ancestors are buried thousands of miles away and you cannot visit their graves, or if the location of their graves is unknown. Seeing photographs or other reminders of your ancestors can give you a daily opportunity to reflect on your own mortality, and strengthen your resolve to live in a way that is ethical, compassionate, and beneficial to all beings, including future generations.

The next two exercises give you options for honoring those who have crossed over, whether that be by visiting their graves or by creating an ancestral altar.

Exercise: Visiting an Ancestor's Grave

Visit the grave of a parent, relative, or ancestor and bring along an offering like flowers or food, as well as a broom or brush for sweeping and gloves for pulling weeds. You may also wish to bring your journal.

Start by cleaning up the site and the surrounding area, then seat yourself near the grave. As you sit quietly, close your eyes and pay close attention to your breathing. Breathe a little slower and more deeply than you ordinarily do. Allow yourself to become fully present in this space.

When you are ready, slowly repeat this phrase, either silently or out loud: "Mother (or Father, or other ancestor), please come to me." Pay attention to any sensations, emotions, thoughts, images, or memories that come into your mind.

Pay attention to the outside world as well. Do you hear or see any birds or animals? Do you overhear a snatch of conversation or glimpse an object in your environment that didn't jump out at you before? Remember, messages from your ancestors can come from inside you *or* outside you, and they can come in many different forms. Give yourself fifteen or twenty minutes to sit and reflect in silence.

If you still don't sense a response from your ancestor after that time, don't feel frustrated. Frustration, annoyance, and impatience all take you out of the receptive mode in which you are best able to connect with your ancestors. Instead, relax. Trust that you will receive messages when you're ready. If you do feel that you have received a message, trust what you have received. It may be a very simple message, or it may not make immediate sense. Either way, just trust it.

When you're ready, write down your experience in your journal, no matter what happened—even if "nothing" happened. If you didn't get a message or it wasn't clear, don't be discouraged. It takes practice to learn to communicate with ancestors who have crossed over. Whether you get a message or not, know that you have honored this ancestor by coming to his or her grave, making an offering, and attempting to make contact.

Thank your ancestor before departing, and make a note in your journal of any dreams you may have that night. Your ancestor may appear to you in that way or use your dreams to send you a message.

Exercise: Creating an Ancestral Altar

Find a space in your home—even a small space will do—that you can dedicate to a family altar. Set a cloth over a table in that area and place photos and other artifacts from your ancestors on it—old letters, jewelry, buttons, or keepsakes. Your altar doesn't need to hold a lot of items—just ones that are significant to you.

You can also add other items that feel beautiful or sacred to you—a vase of flowers, incense, holy water, or anything else that you feel honors those who have crossed over. If you choose, you can certainly add images of religious figures or spiritual teachers. But keep in mind that the primary purpose of this altar is to honor your ancestors.

From time to time, freshen up the altar by moving things around, adding or replacing photos, or arranging fresh flowers. Make a daily or weekly practice of praying to your ancestors as you sit or stand near your altar, and of making regular offerings there. Your altar will soon become a continual reminder of your heritage and of how your ancestors are still active in the lives of their living descendants.

Releasing Earthbound Spirits

Now and then, I encounter a client who is troubled by the presence of an earthbound spirit—usually a relative who crossed over fairly recently but has struggled to let go and make the transition to the next world. Sometimes these spirits may have died years ago but continue to make their presence known. Sometimes they simply have unfinished business of some kind and are attempting to take care of it after death. They typically remain for a few short days, but they may linger much longer, depending on the choices they make.

For four years, I lived in a house in which my entire family could sense a presence. On occasion, we heard noises at night that had no identifiable source. We later learned that the man who had lived there before us had died when he was ninety-two years old after residing there for about fifty years. I received a couple of spirit messages from this man and learned that he just wanted us to take good care of "his" house. I assured him that we would, and he admitted that he liked having a loving family living there. He served as a kind of spiritual sentinel for a couple years, then crossed over of his own accord, trusting that his house was in good hands.

Because they have remained here, earthbound spirits have yet to go through any spiritual evolution, although most will move into the light eventually. There's no reason to be fearful of or alarmed by these presences. They don't remain here to hurt or harm anyone; they often linger for reasons that are very personal. They may have crossed over right before they were about to take an important action or complete an important task. In this case, they may be lingering in the hope that they can somehow complete their mission, even though they no longer have a body. If they suffered a sudden or traumatic death, they may not have had time to fully process the fact that they have died. They may be waiting to "wake up" again, not realizing that it is time for them to leave this plane.

Some earthbound spirits may feel a strong sense of duty or obligation to the people they are leaving behind—for example, a husband leaving behind a widow, or a mother leaving behind a child. These spirits hang around in hopes of protecting those they love, and extending the role they played when they were alive on earth. Spirits who caused harm while they were alive may be reluctant to cross over because they feel shame, or perhaps fear encountering the spirits of those whom they hurt.

Sometimes these earthbound spirits make the transition on their own; sometimes they need a little help from the living in order to move on. The following exercise shows you ways in which you can help these lingering spirits cross over to the other side.

Exercise: Rituals of Release

Techniques for helping earthbound spirits cross over vary depending on the reasons they have for lingering. Use your knowledge about the ancestors in question to make your best guess as to their reasons for staying, then use the corresponding technique to help ease their crossing.

> *Unfinished business*: If you suspect your ancestor is lingering due to unfinished business, ask yourself if you can help them complete that task in some way, whether physically or symbolically. For example, if your ancestor always wanted to see the ocean, take a trip there yourself and leave an offering on their behalf. If your ancestor died in the midst of an important project—writing a novel or organizing the family photos—find a way to bring that project to completion to the best of your ability.

Shock: Ancestors who died suddenly and unexpectedly may still be in shock. If possible, go to the place where they died and tell them the story of what happened to them. Let them know in no uncertain terms that their bodies are gone and that they are free to cross over to the next world. You may even show them a newspaper article, an obituary, or a funeral notice as "proof" that they have died.

Duty: If you suspect that ancestors are lingering out of a sense of duty, ask yourself what you can do to assure them that those they are leaving behind will be okay if they move on. For example, have a long, heartfelt conversation that tells them that you appreciate their love and protection. Assure them that you will be okay and urge them to complete their transition. You can also make a commitment to look after those about whom they may be worried, like a widow or a child.

Shame or fear: If you are aware of a negative action your ancestor performed while here on earth, you may be able to take action on their behalf to move things in a positive direction. For example, if your ancestor was violent toward women, donate money from their estate to a women's shelter. If an ancestor had a long-standing grudge against a neighbor, reach out to that person and express your best wishes for happiness and health. Of course, it is not your job to "fix" your ancestors' wrongdoings, but you can allow them to work through you to make amends within appropriate bounds.

Chapter 12

Ancestral Messengers

As you learned in chapter 5, there are several channels through which you can tune in to ancestral messages. You may perceive these spirit voices as visions or images, as sounds, as sensations, or as intuitions and insights. But no matter how you receive these messages, you still have to be able to interpret them in a way that has meaning for you.

In this chapter, we'll explore two other ways in which you can tune in to spirit voices—animal messengers and dream messengers. Then we'll look at practices that can help you interpret the messages they bring.

Animal Messengers

One of the most common ways the spirit voices of recently departed ancestors come through is in the form of animals. When animals show up in an unusual way or appear repeatedly within a short time frame, it is often because ancestors are trying to communicate with us. If you've ever lost a loved one, you may have felt as if their spirit was sending you a message when you saw a bird, butterfly, or other creature acting in an unusual way—especially if that animal was beloved by the person in life. You may see the real animal, or encounter it in dreams. Or you may notice it in artwork, advertisements, and other places in your visual environment.

One client of mine was devastated when her beloved grandmother died. The day after the funeral, as she was sitting on her patio, a dove alighted on the table. When she looked at it, something in her *knew* that her grandmother had sent this precious little being. The dove's appearance reassured her that her grandmother was doing well. It appeared for the next three days, landing on the same table whenever she sat there.

A couple I know had an intense experience with an animal messenger after their son, Cooper, died in a tragic accident. Even though he was only four years old, he nevertheless became an ancestor once he passed into the spirit realm. In the weeks after his death, their faith in God completely vanished. They were swept away by their grief, trying to adapt to life without their only child.

About four months after his son's passing, as he was driving home from work, the father asked Cooper to send him a sign to let him know that his spirit was near. When he pulled into his driveway, he was shocked to see a full-grown red-tailed hawk sitting there. As he got out of his truck, an inner voice told him to sit down and extend his hand to the bird. When he did, the hawk walked toward him and sat just inches from his hand. Neither he nor the hawk appeared to feel any fear at all. In fact, it felt as if they were two kindred souls sitting and staring at each other in complete amazement.

The man called to his wife to come see what was happening. They were both in awe of the fact that a creature like a hawk would allow them to get so close to it. After the hawk flew away, they did some research on hawks, only to discover that a red-tailed hawk is often referred to as a Cooper's hawk. This hawk reappeared several times over the years, reassuring them that Cooper's spirit was near.

Birds and butterflies seem to be the most common animals ancestors use when they want to make their spirit voices heard—although a friend of mine shared that a dolphin swam close to shore right alongside her as she walked down the beach following her father's death. These animals aren't reincarnations of deceased loved ones; rather, they are messengers or couriers from the spirit world. The messages they bring are usually quite simple and straightforward—for instance, just letting you know deceased loved ones are well and happy. After all, they don't have bodies to contend with—at least not until their souls choose to incarnate again.

In our busy modern lives, we sometimes forget to pay attention to our brothers and sisters in the animal kingdom, or even tune them out—that is, until they send us a message we can't ignore. The next exercise can teach you to pay closer attention to the ways in which birds and other animals show up in your life, whether or not you have recently lost a loved one.

Exercise: Recognizing Animal Messengers

The next time a bird, butterfly, or other animal catches your attention, stop what you are doing and observe it for a few minutes instead of immediately returning to the task at hand. If it's a bird, listen closely to its call. See if you can learn to recognize it by its call even if you can't see it. If it's a butterfly, do some research on its life stages and learn to recognize its caterpillar and cocoon.

Gradually build your knowledge of the birds and animals who call your local environment home until you can reliably identify a dozen or more. The more you learn about the animals in your environment, the more likely you will be to recognize and appreciate the many gifts they bring you—including messages from your ancestors.

Dreams Messengers

As you work with your ancestors, you may find that they begin to show up more frequently in your dreams, giving you messages or simply expressing their gratitude for the work you are doing to heal your ancestral patterns. You may also have dreams related to specific ancestral patterns you are addressing that show you the specific steps you need to take in order to heal.

A woman who participated in one of my ancestral healing workshops spent much of the day working with the spirit of her grandfather. She told me that when she went home that night, she had a dream in which she was walking through the woods and noticed a campfire in the distance. A circle of people were seated around the fire, including an old man who had his back to her. As she approached, she realized that this man was the grandfather with whom she had worked extensively in the workshop. When she got within a few feet of him, he turned and looked straight at her, saying: "Thank you. I can now sit in the circle." She felt a love for him that she had never experienced before and knew that he was grateful for the healing energy she'd sent that day. His spirit voice had come through in her dream.

I've had dreams in which I received messages from recently deceased ancestors, including my father, my mother, my brother, and a nephew who died when he was twelve years old. My father often appears in my dreams to let me know that he's working on my behalf behind the scenes. He is there for me, steering me, advising me—sometimes in ways of which I'm not always conscious, and sometimes in ways of which I'm very aware. He watches over my daughters as well. He once told me in a dream that he felt bad about his drinking and self-destructive behavior while he was on earth. Hearing those words melted my heart, and I experienced a rare instance of total and immediate forgiveness. Although I'd held a grudge for many years about my father's alcoholism, this dream helped me realize that he had suffered a great deal but kept it all inside, hidden under his gruff macho exterior.

When ancestors visit you in dreams, they don't always speak in words that you can understand. They may use gestures or symbols to communicate, or they may utter phrases that seem to make no sense until you take the time to ponder them later. Ancestors may show up in your dreams at the age they were when they died, or they may look younger or older. Sometimes the meaning of a dream will be clear immediately. When this happens, you may feel inspired to take action based on it, or simply make a gesture of gratitude to the ancestors for letting their spirit voices be heard. But sometimes dreams only make sense days or weeks later. When this happens, just trust that their meaning will come if you keep your channels of communication open. And be sure to tune in to all your perceptual channels for additional clues.

Dream Journals

Dream journals have been used since ancient times to record the details of dreams before they slip away. Between 1190 and 1232 CE, a Japanese monk named Myōe recorded all of his dreams on a scroll that now lives at the Metropolitan Museum of Modern Art in New York City. One of these dreams recounts an encounter with a deity at Kasuga Taisha, a Shinto shrine, and includes a sketch of mountains. Some scientists believe the famous cave paintings at Lascaux may actually be the oldest known instance of dream journals, and that dreams, in fact, helped humans evolve into the sophisticated beings we have become.

Ancestral work often has the effect of giving you more frequent and meaningful dreams about the ancestors on whom you've been focusing, or about ancestors you may have been overlooking. In other words, doing the exercises in this book may very likely cause you to have more dreams about your ancestors, and the spirit voices that come through in these dreams can inspire you to focus on certain kinds of healing work. Keeping a dream journal can help you identify patterns over time, and slowly untangle messages that may be mysterious at first.

Exercise: Keeping a Dream Journal

Choose a notebook you will use only for the purpose of recording your dreams, and keep it beside your bed. The next time you have a dream about an ancestor, write down as many details as you can remember as soon as you wake up. Did they appear as the age at which they died? Were they younger? Older? What was their emotional state? What were they doing? Did they speak to you, or use gestures? Note any preliminary interpretations you have of the dream. Is the meaning obvious? Or did the dream leave you searching for answers?

Note the date and time of your dreams, and also note if you'd been thinking about those ancestors or working with them using any of the practices in this book. This can help you identify which practices are more likely to result in dreams, so you can use them more frequently, if that is your intention.

Review your dream journal regularly. Do certain ancestors show up more frequently than others? Does working with a certain practice result in more visits than others? What is the main message your ancestors are sharing with you through your dreams? Listening to the spirit voices of your ancestors in dreams and understanding their meaning can help you move forward toward healing ancestral patterns.

Chapter 13

The Four Gifts

As we saw in chapter 11, many cultures set aside one or more special days during the year on which to honor their ancestors—the Chinese Ghost Festival and Tomb-Sweeping Day, the Buddhist Bon Festival, the Hindu celebration of Pitru Paksha, the Christian observance of All Souls' Day, the ancient Celtic festival of Samhain, and the Mexican Día de los Muertos, to name just a few. On these days, descendants honor those who have crossed over by tending their graves, or bringing them offerings, or setting up home altars.

Some honor their dead on the anniversary of their death or on their birthdays, rather than on a specific holiday. My brother's widow visits his grave every year on his birthday, sometimes accompanied by his children and grandchildren. She always takes along some of his favorite wine, pours them each a glass, and drinks a toast to him. She also brings along one of his favorite dishes to make it a true celebration!

Regardless of which cultural tradition you follow, or the date on which you choose to honor the departed, there are four gifts that the ancestors want to receive from you in your rituals of veneration—acknowledgment, validation, understanding, and forgiveness. If you offer them these four gifts, they will seek to help you in as many ways as possible, serving as spiritual guides and teachers, and acting as both givers and receivers of healing. Although you may find it difficult at first to offer these gifts to your ancestors (or at least to certain ancestors), you will find that it becomes much easier as you work to release ancestral patterns and heal old wounds.

Let's take a look at each of these gifts in more detail.

Acknowledgment means accepting and affirming the truth of your genetic and/or spiritual ties to you ancestors, whether or not you like them or approve of everything they did. You can acknowledge your ancestors by remembering their birthdays and death days, by keeping their memory alive in conversation, by displaying photos of them around the house, or by finding ways to affirm that they existed and continue to exist through you.

Validation means affirming that your ancestors' efforts were not in vain. For example, if your great-great-grandparents were illiterate laborers who worked their fingers to the bone so that your great-grandparents could attend school and learn to read, you can offer them validation by expressing your gratitude for your own literacy. You can also offer them validation by carrying on values that you share with them—for example, generosity, truthfulness, or a strong work ethic.

Understanding means doing your best to see the social, historical, and economic context in which your ancestors lived and appreciating the choices they made—even if those choices seem wrong to you. Engage in dialogue with them and let them know that you perceive their reasons for doing the things they did, within the context of the world in which they lived.

Forgiveness means letting go of any anger, resentment, or ill will you may have borne toward a certain ancestor or group of ancestors. Forgiveness often follows closely in the wake of understanding, because understanding deepens your compassion. You can express your forgiveness to your ancestors by regularly affirming that you release them from any judgments you previously held about them.

Your ability to embody these four gifts will increase the more you work with ancestral healing. The following exercise can help you develop your own ancestor veneration practice that combines all four.

Exercise: Offering the Four Gifts

Start by deciding on a date and time when you will honor your ancestors. This can be as often as every day or as rarely as once a year—for example, on a meaningful anniversary or birthday. Then decide where you will honor them—near an ancestral altar in your home, or at a burial ground or historical site, or at another place that feels meaningful to you.

Choose four small objects to represent acknowledgment, validation, understanding, and forgiveness—for example, a teaspoon of soil from some family land, a flower, a scrap of cloth, a string of beads, an old postage stamp, or a travel ticket. Place these four objects on your altar or by the gravesite one by one. As you do so, call to mind the qualities of acknowledgment, validation, understanding, and forgiveness outlined above. Address a few words to your ancestors to let them know that you are offering them these gifts. As you make your offering, know that your efforts are spreading backward and forward throughout your family line.

Conclude your ritual with any gestures or words that feel meaningful to you, and record the experience in your journal.

Praying for the Ancestors

The word "prayer" is often associated with organized religions like those practiced in a church, a synagogue, or a mosque. But prayer is, in fact, any worshipful speech that invokes the divine qualities of love, forgiveness, healing, and compassion. You don't have to belong to any particular religion or spiritual tradition in order to pray. Indeed, the prayers you write yourself, or those that come to you spontaneously, are often the most powerful.

Prayers can embody all four of the gifts described above. They can be offered as an outpouring of benevolence and understanding, as an act of forgiveness, as acknowledgment and validation, or as healing. When you pray, you assert your own ability to effect change through your loving energy and positive intentions. Although you may begin this next exercise by praying for a specific ancestor, you may soon find yourself expanding your prayers to include all ancestors both known and unknown. Either way, you will experience the tremendous benefits of invoking the four gifts that elevate your own spirit, even as you offer them to your ancestors.

Exercise: Offering an Ancestral Prayer

Assume a posture that feels reverent to you—kneeling, bowing, standing, or extending your palms up. Take a few deep breaths and allow your mind and heart to settle. Feel your higher self taking the reins. Trust that your higher self will provide you with the right words for your prayer.

When you feel ready, begin to speak, either silently or out loud, offering the four gifts to any ancestors you choose. You can name specific ancestors or cast a wide net. If you like, you can request healing for specific conditions, or you can leave your prayer open-ended.

If you feel called, you can offer your forgiveness to a specific ancestor or to your ancestors in general for any pain they have caused. You can also ask for their protection and guidance as you move forward in your life, or express your gratitude for the gifts they have given you.

Allow yourself to speak freely, without hesitation or self-censorship. Feel yourself become a conduit for the qualities of love, forgiveness, and gratitude. When your prayer feels complete, make a ritual gesture that feels meaningful to you, like bowing, clapping your hands, or saying "It is so."

Exercise: Prayer to the Ancestors

This beautiful prayer was written by T. M. Lawson olo Obatala. I've adapted and shortened it for this book:

> I offer light for all my ancestors whose names I know, and all the ones I don't know.

> I offer prayer and protection for those ancestral souls who are in darkness, forgotten, or lost. Let the light I offer fade out the shadows of fear.

Let the light I offer be a beacon of hope and serve as an escape and protective shield from the shadows of despair.

I offer love, compassion, and comfort to those ancestral souls who are suffering and depressed.

I offer healing on all spiritual levels for those ancestors who were abused, afflicted, deceived, enslaved, hated, lonely, misguided, neglected, oppressed, pained, saddened, or traumatized.

Let the light I offer to their souls inspire clemency, liberation, faith, love, and harmony from today onward.

I offer forgiveness to ancestral souls who want to repent sincerely for the error of their ways in the realms of both life and death.

In addition, I forgive those ancestors who committed wrongs that have doomed their generational line to barrenness.

And I forgive those ancestors for whose past sins I've had to suffer as a result of their own naivete, ignorance, or inferior habits and traits. Let the light I offer serve as a reminder for us in the living world to acknowledge and learn not to make the same mistakes as those who lived before us.

In every way, I forgive those ancestors who need it most, so that their souls will embrace in positive gratification a new and improved way of living in the spirit realm, and so those souls will elevate in peace and awaken to eternal life.

Let today be the beginning of a continual healing process for all my ancestral guides.

Let any blocked and negative genetic energy patterns be released.

As you, the Ancestors, heal on the other side, we ask that you forgive us as you have been forgiven. Help us to heal with free-flowing positive and progressive energy for the well-being of all concerned.

Chapter 14

Paying It Forward

I have a friend who is a Cherokee medicine woman. Every morning for the last thirty years, she's gone out on the land on her ranch and communicated with the ancestors. Thanks to this practice, she has realized that much of who we are today began to take form many lifetimes ago. We think of our lives as our own, but the seeds for those lives were planted by the actions and reactions of previous generations. Moreover, she has realized that the lives of future generations will be formed by all of us living today. "That which is healed within one becomes present and available for all," she teaches, "and with each healing, with each release of hurt, pain, wounds, disease, anger, and despair, light will move in to take its place."

These words remind me that we all have the power to bless future generations, ensuring that they inherit light from us instead of pain. Often, when we think about passing things on to our descendants, we think about houses and money and other assets. But we forget that we are also responsible for passing on either a legacy of hurt or an inheritance of love. The more we can heal our own wounds in this life, the fewer wounds we will pass down to future generations—and the healing energy we cultivate will become available to them.

Many spiritual traditions have rituals for blessing newborn children. The following exercise builds on that practice and shows you how to bless all generations still to come and renew your commitment to leave them only light.

Exercise: Blessing Future Generations

Sit in a quiet, comfortable place and close your eyes. If you have children, visualize them sitting in front of you. If you don't have children of your own, you can visualize any children. Then imagine your real or potential grandchildren sitting behind them, and your real or potential great-grandchildren sitting behind them. Visualize as many future generations as you can spreading out ahead of you like waves, with no end in sight.

Call up a feeling of intense love. Feel your entire body fill up with this utterly benevolent energy. Lift your hands with your palms facing out, and send this loving energy flowing out to future generations. Visualize these generations of children being healthy, happy, and free from their ancestors' pain. Know that any light and healing you generate in your own life will benefit them.

Seeding Positive Patterns

Ancestral work often involves a lot of sorrow and catharsis, as you uncover secrets and grieve for the pain caused by old wounds. But this work can also be very joyful, because it reminds you of all the incredible gifts that have been passed down through your family line— gifts that you have the opportunity to pass on to your own descendants. In the years that I've been working with my father as an ancestor, I've had incredible experiences of the love, loyalty, and encouragement that were sometimes difficult for him to convey when he was alive. I've also begun to pay more attention to the positive traits I received from both my parents, as well as from ancestors farther back in time, and to consider the seeds I'd like to plant in my own lineage.

Even if you come from a very dysfunctional family, you probably inherited a few positive traits—perhaps courage, self-sacrifice, thrift, or generosity. Perhaps your ancestral patterns include practical skills that are useful and beneficial to both yourself and others—like knowing how to fix cars, or cook wonderful meals, or speak three languages. Perhaps you carry physical traits like strength or beauty. The more you pay attention to these positive traits and useful skills, the more you can shift your relationship with your ancestors from one of sorrow to one of compassion or even gratitude. You can also begin to tell a new story about your family, one that will open up new possibilities for future generations.

The stories we hear about our ancestors as children have a tremendous impact on how we see ourselves. Those who hear that their ancestors were cruel or stupid, or that their family tree is riddled with intractable curses, may grow up without hope or self-esteem. By emphasizing the positive aspects of our lineage, while acknowledging the healing work still to be done, we can pave the way for future generations to grow into loving ancestors who will, in turn, continue to heal the family line. One way to do this is through positive ancestral affirmations.

Exercise: Positive Ancestral Affirmations

If you've spent your life focusing on the negative aspects of your family heritage, you can seed new truths by creating affirmations that emphasize the positive energies at work in your lineage. Ask yourself what you would like to be true about your family and all future descendants, starting today.

To begin, create a list of three to six qualities you most want to propagate in your family line—for example, loyalty, love, and joie de vivre—then create simple affirmations that describe what you want future generations to be able to say about their family. For example: "My people are loyal," or "I come from a loving family."

Repeat these affirmations every day. Let them sink into your consciousness and imbue your actions with their energy. Know that you are helping to create a positive future for generations yet to come.

Chapter 15

Spiritual and Territorial Ancestors

So far, we've focused on ancestors from your biological and/or adoptive family. These are the ancestors to whom you are related by nature, nurture, or both, and whose impact on your own life is the easiest to see. In this final chapter, I want to broaden our discussion to include spiritual and territorial ancestors—those to whom you are connected by virtue of deep spiritual resonance, or by having lived on the same piece of land. Just like your biological ancestors, these forebears can have a profound impact on your life. They can serve as guides, mentors, and sources of inspiration. Let's take a look at each of these types of ancestors and explore how you can reach out to them to bring their gifts into your life.

Spiritual Ancestors

Spiritual ancestors are those with whom you feel an incredibly powerful resonance, even if they have no genetic connection to you, even if they come from a different land or culture entirely. For example, my Irish friend who was initiated as a sangoma developed a strong spiritual tie to an African shaman who became her mentor and guide. Although he has crossed over, she still maintains an active relationship with him.

I myself have felt a very strong tie to the people and land of Australia, particularly the indigenous cultures that have existed there for well over sixty thousand years. The first time I visited Australia, many years ago, I became fascinated with the didgeridoo, an Aboriginal instrument that produces a deep, rhythmic droning sound punctuated with harmonic overtones. After struggling for a few months to learn how to play this challenging instrument, I heard a voice in my mind that whispered: "Relax. Just breathe. It'll come." After my initial shock, I realized that this spirit voice was that of an Aboriginal spirit guide. Although I was never quite sure of his name, he continued to advise me until I became more proficient in my playing. I now consider this helping spirit to be a spiritual ancestor.

If you have ever felt a strong pull toward a certain land or culture, or toward a spiritual tradition different from the one into which you were born, chances are you have spiritual ancestors waiting to make your acquaintance. Sometimes these inner promptings can be so strong that you feel compelled to travel to a different country, or engage in a course of study or training that calls to you from outside your own culture. The next exercise can help you connect with these ancestors.

Exercise: Meeting Your Spiritual Ancestors

Write in your journal about any ways in which you feel connected to another land or culture. Describe in detail how it makes you feel when you think of that geographic area or tradition, and in what ways you feel connected, whether or not you've actually visited that place. Have you had dreams in which you are dressed in the clothing of that place or tradition? Have you felt drawn to spiritual teachers from other lineages? Do you prefer the music or food from another culture?

Try going on a shamanic journey with the intention of meeting your spiritual ancestors from other cultures, using the basic instructions given in chapter 8.

Territorial Ancestors

In many cultures, it's believed that the Old Ones, the most ancient ancestral spirits, express themselves as natural beings that still inhabit certain regions. These territorial ancestors inhabit a particular geographic area, like a mountain range or a valley. They may show up as guardian spirits of the land their people inhabit. For example, to the Irish, an oak tree isn't "just" a tree—it is also an ancestral spirit that is strongly connected to their homeland. The Aboriginal people of Australia consider Uluru, a large sandstone monolith, to be the home of the ancestors.

Because modern society is so highly mobile, many of us were not raised on the same land on which our biological ancestors lived. Nonetheless, it's important that we respect and honor the territorial ancestors who inhabit the land on which we do live, whether they show up as spiritual beings or physical expressions. These ancestors are likely influencing us, whether we're aware of it or not. You can find out about your territorial ancestors by reading, conducting research online, and requesting guidance from the people around you who have deep ties to the land you inhabit.

This last exercise can help you reach out to and connect with your territorial ancestors.

Exercise: Blessing the Land

The purpose of this ceremony is to bring love, compassion, and other sacred energies to a piece of land by calling on its territorial ancestors, as well as any others who are willing to help.

You can do this at your home or in a public space, as long as you keep the focus on the land itself, not on any buildings or structures on it. Use this ritual to bless the land upon which you walk, whether it's where you live, where you work, or a special place where you spend time. You can do this alone or in a group.

To perform this blessing, you will need:

- Dried herbs suitable for burning, like rosemary or yerba santa

- Loose tobacco, preferably organic

- A quart container filled with water, preferably glass or ceramic

- A soft piece of cloth

- A fireproof container

- A lighter or matches

Place the dried herbs, tobacco, and container of water on the cloth. Raise your hands with your palms open in a receiving position and ask the ancestors to help everyone present be filled with as much light and love as possible. Hold this position, breathing in the energy channeled through the ancestors for a few moments.

Begin to walk slowly around the land you want to bless. As you do so, remember the ancestors who lived there before you. Ask them to help you learn how to live on the land appropriately, and how to remain receptive to their guidance.

When you have completed your walk, return to the cloth and sprinkle the water on the ground, offering your gratitude. Place your herbs in the fireproof container and then light them using a lighter or matches. Allow the smoke to waft over you and the land. Finally, sprinkle the tobacco on the ground as a sign of your respect.

Conclusion

Many years after I embarked on my journey of ancestral healing, I visited a shamanic colleague who asked me if I wanted her to guide a shamanic journey for me. By that point I was already well-acquainted with the tremendous benefits of these journeys, so I eagerly agreed. We went into the special room she had set aside for this purpose. She sat on the floor next to me as I lay down with my eyes closed.

My guide began to play a steady rhythm on a beautiful frame drum and I soon felt myself drifting into an altered state of consciousness. A few minutes later, I found myself sitting up with her behind me and her arms wrapped around me. Something about relaxing back into her very motherly body triggered a deep memory, one for which I had no words at the time. I felt myself spontaneously regress to infancy, then sensed something terribly wrong with my body—as if I were dying. My soul moved out of my infant body and I felt myself going into a tunnel of light. I hurried to get to the opening at the other end of the tunnel and, when I finally got there, I saw a very old ancestor with long, gray hair and a loving smile on his face waiting for me.

I was relieved that this ancestor had come to help me cross over, but when I reached him, he leaned toward me and raised his right hand, with his index finger pointing up. Then he moved his hand from side to side in the universal gesture for "No." He looked straight into my eyes and said very clearly: "Not yet!"

I was shocked and upset by this and pleaded with him, telling him I didn't want to go back. Once again, with that smile on his face, he leaned over and repeated: "Not yet!" I tried a third time without success, then finally turned around and went back the way I'd come. I returned to my body feeling very sad and disappointed.

By this time, my colleague was cradling me as you would a child. I was so grateful for her loving care. I was sobbing as deeply as I ever had in my life, releasing the pain and suffering that my soul knew would be a part of returning to this incarnation called Steven Farmer.

At first I didn't understand why this had happened, but then it hit me. I recalled my mother saying on more than one occasion: "We almost lost you!" She told me that when I was about five months old, I contracted double pneumonia. Since both my parents were now dead, I couldn't ask them to verify whether or not I had technically died, but I know in my heart that I did. It explained so much—how an initiation into a near-death experience at such a young and tender age had set the stage for my future work. It also opened up new dimensions of understanding when it came to my relationship with my parents, who had themselves suffered through the trauma of nearly losing a child.

Ancestral healing work is like this. Just when you think you understand your story, some new piece of information comes to light, revealing insights that may have eluded you before. You may meet new ancestors, or evolve your relationship with the ones you already know. And you start to consider the lives of future generations in everything you do. Even if you walk this path for twenty years, you can always learn new things. The ancestral well is endlessly deep, and so is the amount of good you can do by working skillfully and sincerely with healing practices.

As you work with the practices in this book, know that your experiences with them will evolve over time. New practices will call to you; old practices will exhibit new depths. Messages you thought you understood will reveal fresh layers of meaning. Know that you are always connected to your ancestors, no matter how far you are separated from them by the illusory barriers of space and time. When you focus your attention and open your heart, you will always keep them near.

May you, your ancestors, and your future generations benefit from your healing intentions, just as you are benefiting from theirs.

Acknowledgments

First I'd like to acknowledge all of the ancestors: those who are of our more immediate lineage as well as those elders of the ancestral world, whose lives may be forgotten yet still yield their influence on our lives today. I especially want to thank my father, Richard, and my mother, Helen, for bringing this life that I am into the world. There will be a time when I too will become an ancestor, and in advance of that time I thank my two daughters, Nicole and Catherine, as well as my grandchildren, Jaden, Lila, Desmond, and Golden, for holding me in their memories.

Further thanks to Hierophant Publishing president Randy Davila and his colleague Peter Turner, who inspired this revision so that this book will reach many more people, and to the editorial team at Hierophant Publishing, specifically Hilary, Laurie, and Grace, who all did an excellent job in making this book so readable.

Blessings and thanks to my many friends and family who have served to inspire this and other works with their love, care, and encouragement. I know and trust that my life has been guided by the Spirit Beings that I call my "team," and I know without a doubt that I would not be here were it not for their consistent and powerful messages, insights, and occasional interventions to keep me alive and aligned with my purpose. I am grateful that I have been privileged to create this and other works, and my heart fills with joy and gratitude for all of those who have found these works to inspire and inform!

Appendix A

Therapeutic Modalities
That Support Ancestral Work

If you find that the exercises in this book bring up trauma, intense emotions, or somatic symptoms, I encourage you to seek the support of a therapist, counselor, and/or bodyworker. Here are the specific therapeutic modalities I recommend to support ancestral work. These can all be used in conjunction with the exercises in this book.

This is just a short list of treatment options; there are others available as well that can be just as effective. Do your own research. Talk to practitioners and friends. Find a method or combination of methods that works for you. Keep in mind as well that a method's effectiveness may change over time. So keep things fresh and don't be afraid to try something new.

Hypnotherapy

Hypnotherapy is a set of techniques based in trance states induced by a skilled practitioner. Hypnotherapists make subtle but meaningful suggestions for changes that are in alignment with a client's expressed desires. There are a few different approaches these therapists can employ, but they are all grounded in the premise that it is in the subconscious that these suggestions can take hold, and in turn influence a person's conscious thoughts and behavior. You can find a hypnotherapist in your area by searching the National Board for Certified Clinical Hypnotherapists website at *www.nbcch.com.*

Somatic Experiencing

Somatic experiencing, developed by Peter Levine and described in detail in his book *Waking the Tiger*, is based on the premise that trauma lives in the body. This type of therapy focuses on working with physical symptoms that remain from traumatic experiences. Clients are directed to notice postures and tensions that show up in their bodies, and are guided by therapists to gently release and discharge those tensions. For instance, if a man is talking about being hit as a child and unconsciously raises his hand to his face in a gesture that suggests warding off blows, the therapist will point this out and ask him to repeat this gesture a few times very, very slowly to give his body time to discharge the energy that has been stored.

I did a three-year training in this methodology and found it to be exceptional in deepening my understanding of traumatic experiences and their residual effects. I learned many techniques for treating these wounds. To learn more about somatic experiencing, read *Waking the Tiger* or visit Somatic Experiencing International online at *www.traumahealing.com*.

Eye-Movement Desensitization and Reprocessing (EMDR)

Eye-movement desensitization and reprocessing, or EMDR, was developed by Francine Shapiro, author of *Getting Past Your Past*. When used in a clinical setting, EMDR is a highly useful technique that involves bilateral eye movements—moving your eyes back and forth—while bringing up a disturbing memory. For those who are more auditory, therapists use bilateral clicking sounds. For those who are oriented more to sensation, they use bilateral tapping.

In EMDR sessions, clients start with a disturbing memory and rate it on a scale of one to ten, from least disturbing to most disturbing. They then work with a facilitator to lower the stress level associated with the memory. To learn more about EMDR therapy, visit the EMDR Institute's website at *www.emdr.com*.

Emotional Freedom Technique (EFT)

The Emotional Freedom Technique—also called Tapping—involves clients tapping with their fingers on certain meridian points similar to those used in acupuncture and acupressure while repeating certain phrases that are applicable to the problem at hand. This methodology is proving to be quite effective for treating a number of emotional and psychological conditions, including PTSD. It's a relatively simple technique that, once learned, clients can perform on their own to discharge fear or anxiety. It is not, however, recommended for serious symptoms. To learn more about the Emotional Freedom Technique (EFT), visit *www.eftuniverse.com*.

Breathwork

Several different schools of therapy are based in a fundamental procedure: patterned breathing that induces an altered state of consciousness in which the body-mind spontaneously produces insights and healing. The original technique, called Rebirthing, was developed by

Leonard Orr and is described in his book with Sondra Ray, *Rebirthing in the New Age.*

Holotropic Breathwork, developed by psychiatrist Stanislav Grof, has been one of the more popular evolutions of this tradition. To learn more about Grof and his transpersonal training methods, visit *www.holotropic.com.*

I was trained in a version of breathwork called Vivation that has proven to be very effective. I've used this methodology with clients in the past and recently have seen a resurgence of interest in it. I find it to be a useful tool in my shamanic practice. Vivation uses patterns of breathing that vary from short, rapid breaths to slower deep breathing as the intensity of emotions that surface changes—the more intense the emotions, the more rapid the breathing. Learn more about Vivation at *www.vivation.com.*

Yoga

Yoga is an ancient Hindu discipline that was originally developed to prepare practitioners for death. It has since moved far beyond that original purpose, however. The philosophy and practice of yoga, which has greatly increased in popularity over the years, involves the harmonization of mind, body, and spirit.

Nerve proteins called neuropeptides are key in triggering memories of traumatic events. When the body stays in the flight/flight/freeze mode for a lengthy period of time, this response stays locked in the body. Yoga puts those with PTSD back in their bodies and their breath, and helps to create new and healthier neuropeptide pathways, engaging the parasympathetic nervous system that is responsible for the relaxation response. Beth Shaw describes this process in her article "Trauma Lives in the Body" in *Whole Life Times* magazine, which you can find online at *www.wholelifetimes.com*.

When I first discovered yoga, I was so enthused about it that I took a class every day—sometimes two! Of course, whenever I find something that speaks to my heart, soul, mind, and body, I attack it like a starving man. And this was true when I discovered yoga as well. I encourage you to explore this practice.

Yoga has become very popular in the Western world, and there are several different styles—Ashtanga, Bikram, Hatha, Iyengar, Vinyasa, and others. If this is of interest to you, I suggest sampling different types and classes to see which styles and instructors best suit your needs.

Tai Chi

Tai chi is an ancient Chinese discipline that involves stylized movements coordinated with the breath. The flowing movements express the duality of life—yin and yang, the dynamic/masculine and receptive/feminine—moving from one expression to another of these complementary forces contained within the One. In essence, tai chi is a kind of moving meditation.

I've always been a little too impatient for seated meditation, but once I found tai chi, I worked on learning and practicing the movements for several years. More than once, the 108 movements that constitute the entire sequence left me feeling calm, grounded, and present in body, mind, and spirit. This moving meditation also has a few variations. If tai chi attracts you, search online for a studio or a teacher in your neighborhood.

Family Constellations

Family Constellations is a therapeutic method that draws from a combination of various family systems models. It is designed to help heal unhealthy family patterns and thus aligns well with healing ancestral family patterns. One resource for all kinds of therapeutic practices describes Family Constellations this way:

Family Constellations is an approach for revealing the hidden dynamics in a family so that they can be worked with and healed. Developed by Bert Hellinger, Family Constellation technique involves family representation through the use of others. People are strategically positioned into family roles, including a person in place of the client, in order to bring the family dynamic to fruition. Through non-verbal communication, each member is engaged in a form of cohesive and independent communication that serves to represent the true nature of the family. (*www.goodtherapy.org*)

Although in my psychotherapy days I participated in a number of groups and facilitated similar processes, I've not worked directly with this technique, although I have discussed it with other therapists who feel strongly that it is another means of clearing ancestral family patterns.

Through the interactions of participants, the dysfunctional aspects of families are brought to light for healing. It's reported that those portraying the different family members—including previous generations—are able to express through nonverbal behaviors the thoughts and feelings of those they represent.

Appendix B

Addiction and 12-Step Programs

Addiction of any kind can affect generation after generation of family members, causing untold anguish and shame. Addictions are compulsive activities over which you seem to have no control and that persist in spite of any negative consequences. "Compulsive" here means that you regularly feel an irresistible pull to act on these urges, even if you consciously prefer not to. If you have addiction in your family line, or are aware of having an addiction yourself, I suggest that you seek additional support.

Broadly speaking, there are two kinds of addictions—substance addictions and process addictions. Substance addictions involve things that you ingest, like alcohol, drugs, or food. Process addictions involve behaviors that you act out compulsively, like gambling, sex, or shopping. Paradoxically, these addictions often signify attempts to be in control, even though the behavior itself is out of control.

Some lesser-known process addictions include excessive exercising, an inability to stay away from television or the internet, pornography, work, negativity, cosmetic surgery, and hoarding.

Many people with addictions benefit from 12-step programs like Alcoholics Anonymous. The basic principles of these programs are grounded in four key imperatives:

- Admit that you are powerless over your addiction.

- Identify a higher power that can help you overcome your addiction.

- Identify and make amends to others who have been affected by your addiction.

- Find a new code of ethics by which to live.

For some, regular attendance at and involvement in an appropriate 12-step program is all that is needed for recovery and sobriety. Others may require additional help, perhaps through some of the healing modalities discussed in Appendix A.

If you relate to this in some way, I encourage you to follow through and find an appropriate 12-step program. Commit to six meetings before deciding one way or the other about continuing your participation. Doing this important work will free up the energy you need to do deep ancestral healing.

Appendix C

Index of Exercises

Chapter 1

Building a Family Tree   26

Identifying Ancestral Patterns   28

Appreciating Historical Context   29

Uncovering Ancestral Wounds and Gifts   30

Creating an Ancestral Wish List   33

Chapter 2

Revealing Family Secrets   41

Practicing Self-Reflection   41

Chapter 3

Discovering Your Dark Law   49

Creating Healing Affirmations   50

Changing Your Filter   51

Chapter 4

Exposing Your Headlines   57

Gathering New Perspectives   58

Revising Your Headlines   59

Writing Future Headlines   60

Chapter 5

Finding Your Channel   73

Resolving Interference   74

Chapter 6

Forgiving Yourself   81

Ancestral Dialogue   83

Passing On Forgiveness   85

Chapter 7

Finding the Source   89

Healing a Family Curse   91

Healing Your Descendants   92

What Do You Need to Hear?   96

Ancestral Energy Healing   99

Chapter 8

Journeying to Meet an Ancestor   108

Calling the Ancestors   111

Ancestor Sitting Meditation   114

Chapter 9

Stepping Back to an Elder   119

Embodied Ancestor Healing   124

Chapter 10

Divining with an Ancestor   132

Channeling Spirit Messages   134

Creating an Ancestor Dialogue   137

Past Life Regression   140

Journeying to a Past Life   142

Chapter 11

Imagining Change and Growth   149

Visiting an Ancestor's Grave   153

Creating an Ancestral Altar   155

Rituals of Release   158

Chapter 12

Recognizing Animal Messengers   164

Keeping a Dream Journal   168

Chapter 13

Offering the Four Gifts   174

Offering an Ancestral Prayer   176

Prayer to the Ancestors   177

Chapter 14

Blessing Future Generations   182

Positive Ancestral Affirmations   184

Chapter 15

Meeting Your Spiritual Ancestors   189

Blessing the Land   191

Resources

Abram, David. *The Spell of the Sensuous: Perception and Language in a More-Than-Human World.* New York: Vintage Books, 1997.

"African Ancestral Tradition." *isca-network.org.*

"African Shrines, Altars and Ancestors." June 20, 2001. *www. spirithousesshrines.ucdavis.edu.*

"Ancestor Worship Festivals Around the World." *wikitravel.org.* Last updated October 24, 2014.

"Ancestor Worship in Taoism." *nationsonline.org.*

Arrien, Angeles. *The Four-Fold Way: Walking the Paths of the Warrior, Teacher, Healer and Visionary.* San Francisco: HarperSanFrancisco, 1993.

Becker, Ernest. *The Denial of Death.* New York: Free Press, 1973.

Belic, Roko, writer and director. *Happy*. 2011.

Blum, Ralph H. *The Book of Runes, 25th Anniversary Edition*. New York: St. Martin's Press, 2008.

"Bon Festival." *en.wikipedia.org*. Last updated July 14, 2014.

Boring, Francesca Mason. *Connecting to Our Ancestral Past: Healing Through Family Constellations, Ceremony, and Ritual*. Berkeley, CA: North Atlantic Books, 2012.

Braden, Gregg. *The Divine Matrix: Bridging Time, Space, Miracles, and Belief*. Carlsbad, CA: Hay House, 2007.

Bradshaw, John. *Family Secrets: The Path to Self-Acceptance and Reunion*. New York: Bantam Books, 1995.

"Chinese Ancestor Worship." *religionfacts.com*. Last updated December 16, 2013.

Cowan, Tom. *Shamanism as a Spiritual Practice for Daily Life*. Berkeley, CA: Crossing Press, 1996.

"Family Constellations." *www.goodtherapy.org*. Last updated May 2, 2014.

Furlong, David. *Healing Your Ancestral Patterns: How to Access the Past to Heal the Present.* Malvern, Worcestershire, England: Atlanta Books, 2014.

Harner, Michael. *The Way of the Shaman.* San Francisco: HarperSanFrancisco, 1990.

Hillman, James. *The Soul's Code: In Search of Character and Calling.* New York: Random House, 1996.

Hollis, Karen. "Debunking Earthbound Spirits: When Spirits Stay Behind by Choice, Not Force." *Readings by Karen. www.readingsbykaren.com.*

Ingerman, Sandra. *Soul Retrieval: Mending the Fragmented Self.* San Francisco: HarperSanFrancisco, 1991.

Ingerman, Sandra, and Hank Wesselman. *Awakening to the Spirit World: The Shamanic Path of Direct Revelation.* Boulder, CO: Sounds True, 2010.

Knapp, Joseph. *Ancestral Healing: Gateway to Synchronicity.* Dripping Springs, TX: Blue Lotus Press, 2009.

Kopytoff, Igor. "Ancestors as Elders in Africa." *www.lucy.ukc.ac.uk.*

Lanza, Robert. *Biocentrism: How Life and Consciousness Are the Keys to Understanding the Nature of the Universe.* Dallas, TX: BenBella Books, 2009.

Lawson, T. M. "Ancestral Healing Prayer." *Higher Truths. facebook.com.* Posted on November 13, 2013.

Levine, Peter, with Ann Frederick. *Waking the Tiger: Healing Trauma.* Berkeley, CA: North Atlantic Books, 1997.

MacEowen, Frank. *The Spiral of Memory and Belonging: A Celtic Path of Soul and Kinship.* Novato, CA: New World Library, 2004.

MacKay, Nikki. *The Science of Family: Working with Ancestral Patterns.* Winchester, UK: O Books, 2009.

Narby, Jeremy. *The Cosmic Serpent: DNA and the Origins of Knowledge.* New York: Jeremy P. Tarcher/Putnam, 1998.

Rand, Hollister. *I'm Not Dead, I'm Different: Kids in Spirit Teach Us About Living a Better Life on Earth.* New York: HarperCollins, 2011.

Rich, Judith. "Healing the Wounds of Your Ancestors." *Huffington Post.* April 27, 2011.

Schucman, Helen. *A Course in Miracles, Combined Volume* (Third Edition). Mill Valley, CA: Foundation for Inner Peace, 2007.

Shaw, Beth. "Trauma Lives in the Body: Yoga Helps Vets with PTSD." *WholeLife Times*, April/May 2014.

Somé, Malidoma Patrice. *The Healing Wisdom of Africa: Finding Life Purpose Through Nature, Ritual, and Community*. New York: Jeremy P. Tarcher/Putnam, 1998.

Taylor, Jill Bolte. *My Stroke of Insight: A Brain Scientist's Personal Journey*. New York: Plume, 2006.

Thomas, Ariann. *Healing Family Patterns: Ancestral Lineage Clearing for Personal Growth*. Sedona, AZ: Ancestral Wisdom Press, 2011.

van der Kolk, Bessel, Alexander C. McFarlane, and Lars Weisath, eds. *Traumatic Stress: The Effects of Overwhelming Experience on Mind, Body, and Society*. New York: Guilford Press, 1996.

"Veneration of the Dead." *wikipedia.org*. Last updated July 17, 2014.

Walsh, Roger N. *The Spirit of Shamanism*. New York: Jeremy P. Tarcher, 1990.

Wertz, Richard. "Ancestor Worship." *ibiblio.org*.

Wing, R. L. *The I Ching Workbook*. New York: Doubleday, 1978.

Other Books by the Author

Farmer, Steven D., *Adult Children of Abusive Parents*. Dana Point, CA: Earth Magic Publishing, 2015.

—————. *Animal Spirit Guides: An Easy-to-Use Handbook for Identifying and Understanding Your Power Animals and Animal Spirit Helpers*. Carlsbad, CA: Hay House, 2006.

—————. *Animals: Personal Tales of Encounters with Spirit Animals*. Ft. Lauderdale, FL: Sacred Stories Publishing, 2022.

—————. *Earth Magic: Ancient Shamanic Wisdom for Healing Yourself, Others, and the Planet*. Carlsbad, CA: Hay House, 2009.

—————. *Pocket Guide to Spirit Animals: Understanding Messages from Your Animal Spirit Guides*. Carlsbad, CA: Hay House, 2012.

—————. *Power Animals: How to Connect with Your Animal Spirit Guide*. Carlsbad, CA: Hay House, 2004.

————. *Sacred Ceremony: How to Create Ceremonies for Healing, Transitions, and Celebrations.* Carlsbad, CA: Hay House, 2002.

Card Decks by the Author

Farmer, Steven D. *Children's Spirit Animal Cards.* Palmer Lake, CO: Satiama, 2011.

————. *Earth Magic Oracle Cards: A 48-Card Deck and Guidebook.* Carlsbad, CA: Hay House, 2010.

————. *Messages from the Ancestors Oracle Cards.* San Antonio, TX: Hierophant Publishing, 2021.

————. *Messages from the Spirits of Nature Oracle Cards.* Carlsbad, CA: Hay House, 2022.

————. *Messages from Your Animal Spirit Guides Oracle Cards: A 44-Card Deck and Guidebook.* Carlsbad, CA: Hay House, 2008.

————. *Power Animal Oracle Cards: Practical and Powerful Guidance from Animal Spirit Guides.* Carlsbad, CA: Hay House, 2006.

About the Author

Dr. Steven Farmer is a licensed psychotherapist, shamanic practitioner, hypnotherapist, and trauma recovery specialist with certification in EMDR and Somatic Experiencing. He is the internationally bestselling author of several books and oracle card decks, including *Animals: Personal Tales of Encounters with Spirit Animals, Earth Magic, Animal Spirit Guides, Messages from the Ancestors Oracle Cards,* and *Messages from the Spirits of Nature Oracle Cards.* He offers individual consultations as well as a private mentoring program, and serves on the board of the Society of Shamanic Practice. Visit him at www.drstevenfarmer.com.

San Antonio, TX
www.hierophantpublishing.com